QUOTATIONS

— *Fred Metcalf* —

\B^b\

Biteback Publishing

First published in Great Britain in 2013 by
Biteback Publishing Ltd
Westminster Tower
3 Albert Embankment
London SE1 7SP

Every reasonable effort has been made to trace copyright holders of material
reproduced in this book, but if any have been inadvertently overlooked the
publishers would be glad to hear from them.

ISBN 978-1-84954-225-8

10 9 8 7 6 5 4 3 2 1

A CIP catalogue record for this book is available from the British Library.

Set in Sabon

Printed and bound in Great Britain by
CPI Group (UK) Ltd, Croydon CR0 4YY

CONTENTS

INTRODUCTION

Do you have a sense of humour? Me neither. At least according to my closest friends. I used to have one, until quite recently in fact. But now, after many months spent working on this collection, I have to sadly report that I'm all laughed out. (Or ALO as the young'uns will soon be calling it.)

Doctors of literature are aware of this condition, when nothing seems funny anymore, especially when it's labelled 'humorous'.

Six months ago there was nothing I liked better than a lusty cackle. Today I wake up grimly wailing and mewling.

You know that sound you find yourself emitting after five minutes of listening to a Radio 4 topical 'comedy' show? That sound.

I'm often asked, 'So what sort of people compile this sort of book?'

In my own personal experience, the sort of people who compile 'humorous' books of quotations are a self-selected clerisy of wannabe do-gooders with one simple agenda: to bestow upon the world at large the precious gift of laughter.

It's what we do.

Examine us more closely and you'll find fastidious contextualists, recovering idiots savants, apprentice autodidacts, punsters, funsters, wits and wags.

What a team! Could a world run by such people be worse than the one we have?

As a member of at least three of the above groupings, Dear Reader, I suggest not.

People often ask me, could *I* become a member of this elite band of highly respected humoristas?

Well, it's nice of them to ask, but I'm afraid that membership is by personal recommendation only and we're a little over-subscribed at the moment, but do ask again in a year or two and, well, you never know. Sorry!

One thing that has frequently struck me, as I compiled away, is the similarity between sport and theatre.

There's not a lot of difference. In sport, I suppose, you always know how you've done.

All sport is a form of drama where you don't know the result in advance. Unlike theatre, where you always know how it's going to turn out.

The snooker player Steve Davis once said, 'Sport is cut and dried. You always know when you succeed. You're not an actor. You don't wonder, "Did my performance go down well tonight?"'

There's a little-known show-business condition called *post-performance reassurance syndrome*, which prompts actors and singers to demand instant approval of what they have just done – ideally the moment they leave the stage.

Sportsmen and women don't need to ask, 'How did I do?' They know how they did. They've just come fifth. They've lost. End of story.

I cannot with a clear conscience claim that all the entries – especially those listed under 'Gaffes and Bloopers' – are quoted with 100 per cent accuracy. But I've done my best to ensure that they are.

Many may still be mis-quoted or mis-attributed. Mis-takes will happen.

And where they have, I take full responsibility. In no case are my teammates at Biteback Publishing to blame.

They deserve only praise – and lots of it – for their work in knocking this project into shape.

My heartfelt thanks are due to the team at Biteback. Iain Dale, Lewis Carpenter, Hollie Teague, Namkwan Cho, I'm talking about you. I am exceedingly grateful for all your hard work.

What you are now holding in your hands is the result of many months spent judging, both choosing and pooh-poohing, chuckling and cackling, sifting and sorting.

I hope my efforts have not been in vain. And that my ALO clears up soon.

The high cost to me of bringing glee to you, eh?

The whole thing would be laughable if it wasn't so funny.

Fred Metcalf
June 2013

Fred Metcalf is a jolly good sport, having played for St Sidwell's FC, Exeter School RFC, Lympstone United FC, Dorland Advertising CC, Streatham-Croydon RFC, The David Frost Revue FC, and The Sunday Times FC.

AMERICAN FOOTBALL

When you get old, everything is hurting. When I get up in the morning, it sounds like I'm making popcorn.
Lawrence Taylor, New York Giants linebacker

Pro football is like nuclear warfare. There are no winners, only survivors.
Frank Gifford, American football player and sportscaster

If the FBI went back far enough, I was always suspect: I never liked football.
Father Daniel Berrigan, peace activist, on his release from jail, 1972

Football is not a contact sport. It's a collision sport. Dancing is a good example of a contact sport.
Duffy Daugherty, Michigan State University coach, 1967

To see some of our best-educated boys spending the afternoon knocking each other down, while thousands cheer them on, hardly gives a picture of a peace-loving nation.
Lyndon Baines Johnson, quoted in the *New York Times*, 1967

Football kickers are like taxi cabs. You can always go out and hire another one.
   Buddy Ryan, NFL coach

Woody Hayes doesn't know anything about drugs. He thinks 'uppers' are dentures.
   Archie Griffin, Cincinnati Bengals running back, of player
   and coach

Barkevious Mingo – best football name ever...
   Eric Stangel, TV writer, on defensive end for LSU Tigers,
   2013, tweet

Kai Forbath is also the sound the football just made clanging off the upright.
   Eric Stangel, on Washington Redskins kicker, 2012, tweet

A poll shows that women think men are sexiest playing football. And they're at their least sexy *watching* football.
   Jay Leno, late-night host

Lou is a great talker. If he were God, Moses would have to send out for more tablets.
   Barry Alvarez, player and coach, of retired coach, sports-
   caster and motivational speaker Lou Holtz

I have a lifetime contract. That means I can't be fired during the third quarter if we're ahead and moving the ball.
   Lou Holtz

Just got word of Wes Welker's engagement. Please respect my privacy during this difficult time.
   Allie MacKay, on Wes Welker, wide receiver for New
   England Patriots, 2012, tweet

For a while you're a veteran, and then you're just old.
  Lance Alworth, wide receiver

Losing the Super Bowl is worse than death. With death, you don't have to get up in the morning.
  George Allen, NFL coach

The San Francisco 49ers say they are going to move. They want a new stadium that is more fan friendly. One without a scoreboard.
  Jim Barach, comedy writer

Tom Landry is such a perfectionist that if he were married to Dolly Parton, he'd expect her to cook.
  Don Meredith, quarterback and commentator of player
  and innovative coach

They feature a Buddy Ryan sandwich at his restaurant. It's a little tongue and a lot of baloney.
  Arnie Spanier, radio host

He's Edward Scissorhands. He couldn't catch a cold in Alaska buck naked.
  Emmitt Smith, running back, of Larry Brown,
  running back

The New York Giants announced that seventy-five season ticket holders who threw snowballs during the San Diego game will be banned from attending any more Giant games. I don't think they should be rewarded for that kind of behaviour.
  Conan O'Brien, late-night host

There's this interior lineman who's as big as a gorilla and as strong as a gorilla. If he was as smart as a gorilla, he'd be fine.

Dan Millman, footballer and author

Franco Harris faked me out so bad one time that I got a 15-yard penalty for grabbing my own face mask.

D. D. Lewis, Dallas Cowboys linebacker, of Pittsburgh Steeler

If me and King Kong went into an alley, only one of us would come out. And it wouldn't be the monkey.

Lyle Alzado, NFL defensive end

Mark Gastineau has got an IQ of about room temperature.

Dan Hampton, Chicago Bears defensive tackle, of New York Jets defensive end

Physically, Alonzo Spellman is a world beater. Mentally, he's an egg beater.

Matt Elliott, offensive lineman, of NFL defensive lineman

Place-kickers aren't footballers, they're hired feet.

Alex Karras, footballer, wrestler and actor

Playing middle linebacker is like walking through a lion's cage dressed in a three-piece pork-chop suit.

Cecil Johnson, Tampa Bay Buccaneers linebacker

Terry Bradshaw couldn't spell cat, if you spotted him the 'C' and the 'A'.

Thomas 'Hollywood' Henderson, NFL linebacker, of quarterback and TV analyst

The two most important jobs in America are held by foreigners – room service and goal-kicking.

Beano Cook, college football commentator

When Larry Csonka goes on safari, the lions roll up their windows.

Anon., of fullback

You've heard of people who zig or zag. Well, Elroy 'Crazy Legs' Hirsch also had a zog and a couple of zugs.

Norm Van Brocklin, quarterback, punter and coach, of running back and receiver

It's a good thing William Perry didn't need acupuncture. They'd have to use a harpoon.

Buddy Baron, comedy writer, of gargantuan defensive lineman

William 'The Fridge' Perry is the best use of fat since the invention of bacon.

Ray Sons, *Chicago Sun-Times*, of gargantuan defensive lineman

Football features two of the worst aspects of American life, violence and committee meetings.

George Will, *Newsweek*, 1976

If a man watches three football games in a row, he should be declared legally dead.

Erma Bombeck, American humorist

You have to play this game like somebody just hit your mother with a two-by-four.

Dan Birdwell, defensive lineman for Oakland Raiders

If you're mad at your kid, you can either raise him to be a nose tackle or send him out to play on the freeway. It's about the same.

   Bob Golic, NFL defensive tackle and commentator

A good football coach needs a patient wife, a loyal dog and a great quarterback – but not necessarily in that order.

   Bud Grant, head coach of Minnesota Vikings

Coach Jim Walden has the Midas touch – everything he touches turns to mufflers.

   Steve Raible, Seattle Seahawks wide receiver and
   commentator

I'd catch a punt naked in the snow in Buffalo for a chance to play in the NFL.

   Steve Hendrickson, NFL linebacker

San Francisco has always been my favorite booing city. I don't mean the people boo louder or longer, but there is a very special intimacy. When they boo you, you know they mean *you*. Music, that's what it is to me. One time in Kezar Stadium they gave me a standing boo.

   George Halas, player, coach, owner with Chicago Bears

American football makes rugby look like a Tupperware party.

   Sue Lawley, English broadcaster, 1985

Rugby is a beastly game played by gentlemen. Soccer is a gentleman's game played by beasts. Football is a beastly game played by beasts.

   Henry Blaha, American sports journalist, 1972

Football is, after all, a wonderful way to get rid of aggressions without going to jail for it.
Heywood Hale Broun, *Tumultuous Merriment*, 1979

Football is a game of clichés and I believe in every one of them.
Vince Lombardi, American football coach

We didn't lose the game; we just ran out of time.
Vince Lombardi

Football builds self-discipline. What else would induce a spectator to sit out in the open in sub-freezing weather?
Anon.

There are several differences between a football game and a revolution. For one thing, a football game usually lasts longer and the participants wear uniforms. Also, there are usually more casualties in a football game. The object of the game is to move a ball past the other team's goal line. This counts as six points. No points are given for lacerations, contusions, or abrasions, but then no points are deducted, either. Kicking is very important in football. In fact, some of the more enthusiastic players even kick the ball, occasionally.
Alfred Hitchcock, film director

See also: CHEERLEADERS, COLLEGE FOOTBALL

ARCHERY

It was a 10 when it left the bow!
    Anon.

To be sure of hitting the target, shoot first and whatever you hit, call it the target.
    Anon.

Archery is 1 per cent form, 2 per cent concentration and 97 per cent DUMB LUCK!
    Anon.

Advice for Archers:
Stalk softly and carry a bent stick.
    Anon.

It's always farther out of the woods than it is into the woods.
    R. T. Turk, veteran archer

Where'd all them Indians come from?
    General Custer, 1876

ATHLETICS

I wasn't a very athletic boy. I was once lapped in the long jump.
  Ronnie Corbett, comedian

What will my country give me if I win 100 metres gold in Sydney? Tobago probably.
  Ato Boldon, Trinidad and Tobago sprinter

A proper definition of an amateur sportsman today is one who accepts cash, not cheques.
  Jack Kelly, reporter

The pain while running is equivalent to the pain of being tickled too much. It hurts but it is still enjoyment.
  Lolo Jones, American Olympic hurdler, 2012, tweet

I wouldn't be surprised if one day Carl's halo slipped and choked him.
  Allan Wells, British sprinter, of American sprinter Carl Lewis

Only think of two things – the gun and the tape. When you hear the one, just run like hell until you break the other.
  Sam Mussabini, South African athletics coach

Running is an unnatural act, except from enemies and to the bathroom.

Anon.

I became a great runner because if you're a kid in Leeds and your name is Sebastian, you've got to become a great runner.

Sebastian Coe, British runner

From what I understand, these drugs shrink your nuts. I can't have my thingy shrunk. I can't afford that!

Kim Collins, West Indian sprinter, on why he would never take banned drugs

I did the 100 metres in eight seconds.
But the world record holder can only do it in ten seconds!
Yes, but I know a short cut!

Anon.

Linford Christie: the generously-beloined sprint supremo.

Punch

It always makes me laugh.
It's such a puzzling treat,
To see an athlete run a mile,
And only move two feet.

Anon.

You have to be suspicious when you line up against girls with moustaches.

Maree Holland, Australian athlete

If Diane Modahl was forty times over the testosterone limit, she'd have a deep voice and we'd all be calling her Barry White.

Tony Jarrett, English sprinter, on the Modahl drug allegations, 1994

It should not have surprised anyone that Ben Johnson was using steroids. You don't go from 10.17 [seconds] to 9.83 on unleaded gas.

Jamie Astaphan, doctor, supplier of steroids to Ben Johnson

Ben Johnson must still be the fastest human in the world. He served a lifetime sentence in only two years.

Mike Littwin, American journalist, after Johnson's life ban was lifted

On Sing Sing Prison's athletics day: we do not have cross-country and we do not have pole vaulting.

Gerald Curtin, sports director at Sing Sing

The French cannot produce great track-and-field teams like they can produce great wines for probably that reason: the winemakers got in first.

Michael Lourie

GAFFES AND BLOOPERS

This is a double disaster, because the last thing anyone wants to see is Irina Korzhanenko stripped.

Gavin McDougald, journalist, after the Russian shot putter was stripped of her Olympic gold medal

Zola Budd, so small, so waif-like, you literally cannot see her. But there she is.
   Alan Parry, commentator

She's really tough; she's remorseful.
   David Moorcroft, runner and commentator

Harvey Glance, the black American sprinter, with the white top and the black bottom.
   Ron Pickering, commentator

Watch the time. It gives you a good indication of how fast they are running.
   Ron Pickering

Ian Mackie is here to prove his back injury is behind him.
   Anon., of Scottish sprinter

I just want to get back to the shape I'm in now.
   Jamie Baulch, British sprinter

She hasn't run faster than herself before.
   Zola Budd, South African runner

The decathlon is nine Mickey Mouse events and the 1,500 metres.
   Steve Ovett, runner and commentator

As a runner Daley Thompson is excellent, as a jumper he is excellent, and as a thrower he is an excellent runner and jumper.
   Cliff Temple, commentator, on decathlete

When I lost my decathlon world record I took it like a man. I only cried for ten hours.

> Daley Thompson, British decathlete

Seb Coe is a Yorkshireman. So he's a complete bastard and will do well in politics.

> Daley Thompson, on middle-distance runner

The Kenyans haven't done much in the last two Games. In fact, they haven't competed since 1972.

> Brendan Foster, British runner and commentator

When you go into an indoor championships like this, it's different to the outdoors.

> Max Jones, athletics administrator

Derek, tell us about your amazing third leg.

> Ross King, broadcaster, to English relay runner Derek Redmond

Is there something that sticks out that makes you an exceptional pole-vaulter?

> Adrian Chiles, broadcaster

For Linford Christie to get the job he'll have to prove whiter than white.

> Victoria Derbyshire, broadcaster

And finally she tastes the sweet smell of success.

> Ian Edwards, cross-country runner

David Coleman – British Sports Commentator

A fascinating duel between three men.

A truly international field, no Britons involved.

Alan Pascoe could have won the gold, but he simply ran out of time.

He was dead before he hit the floor and he never regained consciousness.

And here's Moses Kiptanui – the nineteen-year-old Kenyan who turned twenty a few weeks ago.

And the line-up for the final of the women's 400 metres hurdles includes three Russians, two East Europeans, a Pole, a Swede and a Frenchman.

And with an alphabetical irony, Nigeria follows New Zealand.

As they come through absolutely together with Wells in first place.

Bradford, who has gone up from 200 metres to 400, found it hard going and for the last 100 metres was always going backwards.

Charlie Spedding believes in an even pace and hopes to run the second part of the race faster than the first.

Coe has made absolutely no move at all down the back straight.

David Bedford is the athlete of all time in the 1970s.

He is accelerating all the time. The last lap was run in sixty-four seconds and the one before in sixty-two.

He is even smaller in real life than he is on the track.

He just can't believe what's not happening to him.

He won the bronze medal in the 1976 Olympics so he is used to being out in front.

He's thirty-one this year. Last year he was thirty.

Her time was four minutes thirty-three seconds, which she is capable of.

Here are some names to look forward to, perhaps in the future.

His brother failed, so let's see if he can succeed and maintain the family tradition.

In a moment we hope to see the pole vault over the satellite.

Ingrid Kristiansen has smashed the world record, running the 5,000 metres in 14:58:09. Truly amazing. Incidentally this is a personal best for Ingrid Kristiansen.

It doesn't mean anything, but what it does mean is that Abdi Bile is very relaxed.

It's a battle with himself and the ticking finger of the clock.

It's a great advantage to be able to hurdle with both legs.

It's gold or nothing ... and it's nothing. He comes away with the silver medal.

Lasse Virén, the champion, came in fifth and ran a champion's race.

Lillian Board's great strength is her great strength.

Morcelli has the four fastest 1,500-metre times ever. And all those times are at 1,500 metres.

One of the great unknown champions, because very little is known about him.

Panetta was the silver medallist in the European Championships when he led all the way.

She's not Ben Johnson, but then, who is?

That's the fastest time ever run, but it's not as fast as the world record.

The big guns haven't pulled all the stops out.

The late start is due to the time.

The news from the javelin is that it was won by the winning throw that we saw earlier.

The reason why she's so fast over hurdles is because she's so fast between them.

The Republic of China – back in the Olympic Games for the first time.

There is Brendan Foster, by himself with 20,000 people.

There you can see her parents. Her father died some time ago.

There'll be only one winner in every sense of the word.

There's going to be a real ding-dong when the bell goes.

This could be a repeat of what will happen at the European games next week.

This is a young man who is only twenty-five, and you have to say, he has answered every question that has ever been asked.

This man could be a dark horse.

This race is all about racing.

We estimate, and this isn't an estimation, that Grete Waitz is eighty seconds behind.

You've got to hand it to Gonzales. Once he saw it was possible, he saw his chance and made it possible.

Fiona May lost out on the gold medal only because the Spanish athlete jumped further than she did.

See also: MARATHON, OLYMPICS, TRACK AND FIELD

AUSTRALIAN RULES FOOTBALL

Australian Rules Football might best be described as a game devised for padded cells, played in the open air.
  Jim Murray, American sportswriter

I want to kick seventy or eighty goals this season, whichever comes first.
  Barry Hall, Sydney Swans

Apart from their goals, St Kilda was scoreless in that opening quarter.
  Eddie McGuire, Australian sports commentator

More football later, but first let's see the first-half highlights from the Essendon vs. Collingwood game.
  Peter Landy, Australian television presenter

He's a guy who gets up at six o'clock in the morning regardless of what time it is.
  Kevin Sheedy, player and coach, of James Hird, player
  and coach

Without giving offence to anyone, I may remark that it is a game which commends itself to semi-barbarous races.
  Edward Kinglake, *The Australian at Home*, 1891

BADMINTON

Ernie: Excuse me, won't you – I'm a little stiff from badminton.
Eric: It doesn't matter where you're from.
  Eric Morecambe and Ernie Wise, *The Morecambe and Wise Joke Book*, 1979

BASEBALL

Are you excited about the opening of the baseball season? Ah, the leather, the pine tar, the rosin – and that's just the hot dogs.

Conan O'Brien, late-night host

Baseball is a skilled game. It's America's game – it, and high taxes.

Will Rogers, wit

Baseball is a game which consists of tapping a ball with a piece of wood, then running like a lunatic.

H. J. Dutiel, wit

Baseball has the great advantage over cricket of being sooner ended.

George Bernard Shaw, Irish playwright

In our team we have so few hits that if anyone reaches first base, he has to stop and ask the way.

Anon.

My team's lost so many games that when it rains, we have a victory party!

Anon.

Getting a ball past his bat is like trying to sneak the sun past a rooster.

Anonymous pitcher on Hank Aaron, 1973

A baseball game is simply a nervous breakdown divided into nine innings.

Earl Wilson, columnist

A friend got me seats to the World Series. From where I sat, the game was just a rumour.

Henny Youngman, comedian

A good cigar is like a beautiful chick with a great body who also knows the American League box scores.

M*A*S*H, sitcom, 'Bug-Out', 1976

Every time a baseball player grabs his crotch, it makes him spit. That's why you should never date a baseball player.

Marsha Warfield, actress and comedienne

The only good thing about playing for Cleveland is you don't have to make road trips there.

Richie Scheinblum, outfielder for Cleveland Indians

Ted Simmons didn't sound like a baseball player. He said things like 'Nevertheless' and 'If, in fact'.

Dan Quisenberry, relief pitcher

Losing is the bane and bugbear of every professional athlete's existence, but in baseball the monster seems to hang closer than in other sports, its chilly claws and foul breath palpable around the neck hairs of the infielder bending for his crosshand scoop or the reliever slipping his first two fingers off-center on the ball seams before delivering his two-and-two cut fastball.

Roger Angell, *Baseball*, 1994

He wants Texas back.

Tommy Lasorda, when asked during contract negotiations with Mexican-born Fernando Valenzuela what the pitcher might demand

The Houston Astros play in a vast indoor stadium known as the Astrodome, but the problem is they field a half-vast team.

Kurt Bevacqua, Major League Baseball player

Haven't they suffered enough?

Beano Cook, college football commentator, on giving free Major League passes to former Iranian hostages

Baseball is like church. Many attend, but few understand.

Wes Westrum, player, coach, manager and scout

It was so foggy today that the Cubs couldn't even see who was beating them.

Anon.

When [Athletics' owner] Charlie Finley had his heart operation, it took eight hours – seven and a half to find his heart.

Steve McCatty, Oakland Athletics pitcher

Fernando Valenzuela is the pitcher whose name sounds like a mailing address in the Lower Andes.

Tom Boswell, sportswriter

Harvey Kuenn's face looks like it could hold three days of rain.

Tommy Lasorda, player and manager of Brooklyn/Los
Angeles Dodgers, of player, coach and manager

If it's true you learn by your mistakes, Jim Frey will be the best manager ever.

Ron Luciano, Major League umpire

When I started, the game was played by nine tough competitors on grass, in graceful ballparks. But while I was trying to answer the daily quiz Quiz-O-Gram on the exploding scoreboard, a revolution was taking place around me. By the time I finished, there were ten men on each side, the game was played indoors on plastic, and I had to spend half my time watching out for a man dressed in a chicken suit who kept trying to kiss me.

Ron Luciano

The first thing they do in Cleveland, if you have talent, is trade you for three guys who don't.

Jim Kern, retired pitcher and three-time American League
All-Star

Major League Baseball has asked its players to stop tossing baseballs into the stands during games, because they say fans fight over them and they get hurt. In fact, the Florida Marlins said that's why they never hit any home runs. It's a safety issue.

Jay Leno, late-night host

Manny Ramirez is a comically awful outfielder. He is a tremendous hitter but he couldn't catch radiation poisoning at a KGB reunion banquet.

Angus Hamilton, of Dominican outfield and designated hitter

He'd give you the shirt off his back. Of course, he'd call a press conference to announce it.

Catfish Hunter, right-handed pitcher, of right-fielder
Reggie Jackson

The designated gerbil.

Bill Lee, of Don Zimmer, infielder, manager and coach

Could be that Bill Terry's a nice guy when you get to know him, but why bother?

Dizzy Dean, pitcher and commentator, of first baseman
and manager

The one thing that kept Jack Perconte from being a good Major League player is performance.

Del Crandall, catcher and manager, of second baseman

Say, Satch, tell me, was Abraham Lincoln a crouch hitter?

Lefty Gomez, New York Yankees pitcher, to veteran
Satchel Paige

The Cleveland Indians traded infielder Stubby Clapp for a player to be named better.

Bud Geracie, sportswriter

Buddy Bell says the two biggest career shorteners are hustle and sweat. Oh, Buddy hustles, but he hustles at his own pace. He's a slow hustler. The biggest thing Buddy does all winter is renew his subscription to *TV Guide*.

    Rich Donnelly, Major League coach, of third baseman
    and manager

He's even-tempered. He comes to the ballpark mad – and stays that way.

    Joe Garagiola Sr, catcher and announcer, of Rick Burleson,
    famously intense Major League shortstop

Mickey Hatcher is the first player to make the major leagues on one brain cell.

    Roy Smalley Jr, Major League shortstop

Danny Napoleon's so ugly that when a fly ball is hit towards him, it would curve away from him.

    Mickey Rivers, center fielder, of Major League outfielder

If you put his brain in a blue jay, the bird would fly backwards.

    Al Nipper, former pitcher and coach, of Mitch Williams,
    relief pitcher and analyst

In a recent survey only 13 per cent of Americans said that baseball was their favourite sport. The survey was taken in the Mets dugout.

    Conan O'Brien

When he laughs, he makes dogs whine.
  Lindsey Nelson, sportscaster, of Tom Seaver,
  celebrated pitcher

Nothing is more limited than being a limited partner of George Steinbrenner.
  John McMullen, former Yankees co-owner

Gene Mauch's stare can put you on the disabled list.
  Tim McCarver, catcher and sportscaster, of player
  and manager

His limitations are limitless.
  Danny Ozark, Phillies coach and manager, of outfielder
  Mike Anderson

Leo Durocher has the ability of taking the bad situation and making it immediately worse.
  Branch Rickey, baseball executive, of infielder and manager

Tommy Lasorda will eat anything as long as you pay for it.
  Joe Torre, player, manager and executive

Mario Soto had a million-dollar arm and a ten-cent head.
  Alex Trevino, Mexican catcher, of Cincinnati Reds pitcher

We've got a problem here. Luis Tiant wants to use the bathroom, and it says no foreign objects in the toilets.
  Graig Nettles, third baseman, on the Cuban pitcher

Robert 'Lefty' Grove could throw a lamb chop past a wolf.
  Arthur 'Bugs' Baer, New York journalist and humorist, on
  Boston Red Sox pitcher

A hot dog at the ballgame beats roast beef at the Ritz.
  Humphrey Bogart, actor

Harmon Killebrew has enough power to hit home runs in
any park – including Yellowstone.
  Paul Richards, catcher, manager and scout

There is nothing remarkable about throwing or catching or
hitting a ball. Jugglers in Yugoslavia do it better.
  Jim Murray, sportswriter for *Los Angeles Times*

Baseball is the favourite American sport because it's so slow.
Any idiot can follow it. And just about any idiot can play it.
  Gore Vidal, American novelist

Call me un-American; call me Canadian or Swedish, I don't
care. I hate baseball ... I have lots of reasons to hate baseball. For one it's dull. Nothing happens. Watching baseball
is like going to a lecture by a member of the Slow ... Talkers
... of ... America. It's like turning on the TV – when the cable
is out. It's like watching grass – no – Astroturf grow.
  Jeff Jarvis, American journalist, *Entertainment Weekly*

The underprivileged people of the Americas play some
strange game with a bat which looks like an overgrown
rolling pin.
  Fred Trueman, English cricketer

Calling it the World Series must impress the world as an
example of America's modesty.
  Anon.

You remember baseball? A sort of razzamatazz rounders, played by rowdy roughnecks, wielding oversized clubs and oversized tennis balls.

Rob Steen, British sports journalist

They've played on grass and they've played on Astroturf. What they should do is put down a layer of paper in Candlestick Park. After all, the Giants always look good on paper.

Don Rose, radio personality, on San Francisco's stadium

The sneer is gone from Casey's lip, his teeth are clenched in hate;
He pounds with cruel violence his bat upon the plate.
And now the pitcher holds the ball, and now he lets it go,
And now the air is shattered by the force of Casey's blow.

Oh, somewhere in this favored land the sun is shining bright;
The band is playing somewhere, and somewhere hearts are light,
And somewhere men are laughing, and somewhere children shout;
But there is no joy in Mudville – mighty Casey has struck out.

Ernest Lawrence Thayer, 'Casey at the Bat', *San Francisco Examiner*, 1888

Baseball is a fun game. It beats working for a living.

Phil Linz, backup infielder

Baseball is a game where a curve is an optical illusion, a screwball can be a pitch or a person, stealing is legal and you can spit anywhere you like except in the umpire's eye or on the ball.

Jim Murray

Baseball is the only field of endeavor where a man can succeed three times out of ten and be considered a good performer.

Ted Williams, player and manager, Boston Red Sox

Baseball is the only major sport that appears backwards in a mirror.

George Carlin, *Brain Droppings*, 1997

Baseball is the only sport I know that when you're on offense, the other team controls the ball.

Ken Harrelson, *Sports Illustrated*, 1976

Baseball was made for kids, and grown-ups only screw it up.

Bob Lemon, pitcher and manager

Every hitter likes fastballs, just like everybody likes ice cream. But you don't like it when someone's stuffing it into you by the gallon. That's what it feels like when Nolan Ryan's throw'n' balls by you.

Reggie Jackson, right fielder

I don't want to play golf. When I hit a ball, I want someone else to go chase it.

Rogers Hornsby, infielder, manager and coach

I see great things in baseball. It's our game – the American game. It will take our people out-of-doors, fill them with oxygen, give them a larger physical stoicism. Tend to relieve us from being a nervous, dyspeptic set. Repair these losses, and be a blessing to us.

Walt Whitman, poet

If a woman has to choose between catching a fly ball and saving an infant's life, she will choose to save the infant's life without even considering if there are men on base.

Dave Barry, *Miami Herald*

I'm convinced that every boy, in his heart, would rather steal second base than an automobile.

Tom Clark, sports journalist

It's hard to win a pennant, but it's harder losing one.

Chuck Tanner, left fielder and manager

No game in the world is as tidy and dramatically neat as baseball, with cause and effect, crime and punishment, motive and result, so cleanly defined.

Paul Gallico, novelist

People ask me what I do in winter when there's no baseball. I'll tell you what I do. I stare out the window and wait for spring.

Rogers Hornsby

Poets are like baseball pitchers. Both have their moments. The intervals are the tough things.

Robert Frost, poet

That's baseball, and it's my game. Y' know, you take your worries to the game, and you leave 'em there. You yell like crazy for your guys. It's good for your lungs, gives you a lift, and nobody calls the cops. Pretty girls, lots of 'em.

Humphrey Bogart

There are three things in my life which I really love: God, my family, and baseball. The only problem – once the baseball season starts, I change the order around a bit.

Al Gallagher, third baseman

What is both surprising and delightful is that spectators are allowed, and even expected, to join in the vocal part of the game... There is no reason why the field should not try to put the batsman off his stroke at the critical moment by neatly timed disparagements of his wife's fidelity and his mother's respectability.

George Bernard Shaw

When we played softball, I'd steal second base, feel guilty and go back.

Woody Allen, comedian

When you're in a slump, it's almost as if you look out at the field and it's one big glove.

Vance Law, third baseman

With those who don't give a damn about baseball, I can only sympathize. I do not resent them. I am even willing to concede that many of them are physically clean, good to their mothers and in favor of world peace. But while the game is on, I can't think of anything to say to them.

Art Hill, writer, on baseball

You gotta be a man to play baseball for a living, but you gotta have a lot of little boy in you, too.

Roy Campanella, catcher

You see, you spend a good piece of your life gripping a baseball, and in the end it turns out that it was the other way around all the time.

Jim Bouton, *Ball Four*, 1970

A ballplayer's got to be kept hungry to become a big-leaguer. That's why no boy from a rich family ever made the big leagues.

Joe DiMaggio, New York Yankee, quoted in the *New York Times*, 1961

Baseball is almost the only orderly thing in a very un-orderly world. If you get three strikes, even the best lawyer in the world can't get you off.

Bill Veeck, franchise owner and promoter

If a horse can't eat it, I don't want to play on it.

Dick Allen, Major League Baseball player, on artificial turf

It breaks your heart. It is designed to break your heart. The game begins in spring, when everything else begins again, and it blossoms in the summer, filling the afternoons and evenings, and then as soon as the chill rains come, it stops and leaves you to face the fall alone.

A. Bartlett Giamatti, 'The Green Fields of the Mind', *Yale Alumni Magazine*, 1977

The charm of baseball is that, dull as it may be on the field, it is endlessly fascinating as a rehash.

Jim Murray

I was the worst hitter ever. I never even broke a bat until last year when I was backing out of the garage.

Lefty Gomez

The designated hitter rule is like letting someone else take Wilt Chamberlain's free throws.

Rick Wise, right-hand pitcher

Watching a spring training game is as exciting as watching a tree form its annual ring.

Jerry Izenberg, sports journalist

Wives of ballplayers, when they teach their children their prayers, should instruct them how to say: 'God bless Mommy, God bless Daddy, God bless Babe Ruth. Babe Ruth has upped Daddy's paycheck by 15 to 40 per cent.'

Waite Hoyt, Major League Baseball pitcher

A baseball fan has the digestive apparatus of a billy goat. He can, and does, devour any set of diamond statistics with insatiable appetite and then nuzzles hungrily for more.

Arthur Daley, *New York Times* sportswriter

A critic once characterized baseball as six minutes of action crammed into two-and-one-half hours.

Ray Fitzgerald, *Boston Globe*, 1970

Baseball is an allegorical play about America, a poetic, complex, and subtle play of courage, fear, good luck, mistakes, patience about fate, and sober self-esteem.

Saul Steinberg, *New Yorker* cartoonist

Baseball is not necessarily an obsessive–compulsive disorder, like washing your hands 100 times a day, but it's beginning to seem that way. We're reaching the point where you can be a truly dedicated, state-of-the-art fan or you can have a life. Take your pick.

Thomas Boswell, *Washington Post*, 1990

During my eighteen years I came to bat almost 10,000 times. I struck out about 1,700 times and walked maybe 1,800 times. You figure a ballplayer will average about 500 at bats a season. That means I played seven years without ever hitting the ball.

Mickey Mantle, center fielder for New York Yankees

It's no coincidence that female interest in the sport of baseball has increased greatly since the ballplayers swapped those wonderful old-time baggy flannel uniforms for leotards.

Mike Royko, Chicago newspaper columnist

I've come to the conclusion that the two most important things in life are good friends and a good bullpen.

Bob Lemon

No matter how good you are, you're going to lose one-third of your games. No matter how bad you are you're going to win one-third of your games. It's the other third that makes the difference.

Tommy Lasorda

Sandy's fastball was so fast some batters would start to swing as he was on his way to the mound.

Jim Murray, on Sandy Koufax, left-handed pitcher for
Brooklyn/Los Angeles Dodgers

That's the true harbinger of spring, not crocuses or swallows returning to Capistrano, but the sound of a bat on a ball.

Bill Veeck

The pitcher has to find out if the hitter is timid. And if the hitter is timid, he has to remind the hitter he's timid.

> Don Drysdale, Los Angeles Dodgers right-handed pitcher,
> quoted in the *New York Times*, 1979

The strongest thing that baseball has going for it today are its yesterdays.

> Lawrence Ritter, American writer

This is a game to be savored, not gulped. There's time to discuss everything between pitches or between innings.

> Bill Veeck

The tradition of professional baseball always has been agreeably free of chivalry. The rule is, 'Do anything you can get away with.'

> Heywood Broun, sportswriter and columnist

Say this for big league baseball – it is beyond any question the greatest conversation piece ever invented in America.

> Bruce Catton, American journalist

I'm throwing twice as hard as I ever did. The ball's just not getting there as fast.

> Lefty Gomez

The more we lose, the more he'll fly in. And the more he flies in, the better the chance there'll be a plane crash.

> Graig Nettles, on George Steinbrenner, principal owner of
> the New York Yankees for thirty-seven years

The most overrated underrated player in baseball.

> Larry Ritter, on Tommy Henrich

Some of our hitters are so bad that they can strike out on two pitches.

  Milton Berle, comedian

Baseball must be a great game to survive the people who run it.

  Arthur Daley

It's a good thing I stayed in Cincinnati for four years; it took me that long to learn how to spell it.

  Rocky Bridges, utility infielder

The runners have returned to their respectable bases.

  Dizzy Dean

The clock doesn't matter in baseball. Time stands still or moves backward. Theoretically, one game could go on forever.

  Herb Caen, San Francisco columnist

What does Mama Bear on the pill have in common with the World Series? No cubs.

  Skip Caray, sportscaster, on Chicago's lack of success

How can we keep the [Atlanta] Braves on their toes? Raise the urinals.

  Darrel Chaney, Braves player and announcer in Major
  League Baseball

When we [England] have a World Series, we ask other countries to participate.

  John Cleese, comedian

I made a game effort to argue but two things were against me: the umpires and the rules.

Leo Durocher

I never questioned the integrity of an umpire. Their eyesight, yes.

Leo Durocher

I believe in rules. Sure I do. If there weren't any rules, how could you break them?

Leo Durocher

I've seen better hands on a clock.

Mel Durslag, LA sports columnist, on clumsy shortstop
Bill Russell

I told Roland Hemond to go out and get me a big-name pitcher. He said, 'Dave Wehrmeister's got eleven letters. Is that a big enough name for you?'

Eddie Eichorn, Chicago White Sox owner

A baseball park is the one place where a man's wife doesn't mind his getting excited over somebody else's curves.

Brendan Francis, broadcaster

I don't put any foreign substances on the baseball. Everything I use is from the good old USA.

George Frazier, pitcher and commentator

They shouldn't throw that at me. I'm the father of five or six kids!

Tito Fuentes, Cuban second baseman

Billy Loes [Dodgers pitcher] was the only player in the majors who could lose a ground ball in the sun.
  Joe Garagiola, player and, later, announcer

Nolan Ryan is pitching much better now that he has his curve-ball straightened out.
  Joe Garagiola

When Neil Armstrong first set foot on the moon, he and all the space scientists were puzzled by an unidentifiable white object. I knew exactly what it was. That was a home run hit off me in 1937 by Jimmie Foxx.
  Lefty Gomez

If it turns out that Barry Bonds used steroids to bulk up and add muscle mass, he could get four to eight years as governor of California.
  Argus Hamilton, comedian, on Pittsburgh Pirates and San
  Francisco Giants outfielder. Bonds was a central figure in
  baseball's steroids scandal

Crowd? This isn't a crowd. It's a focus group!
  Fran Healy, disappointed by the poor attendance at a game
  in Montreal

I wish I could play Little League now. I'd be way better than before.
  Mitch Hedberg, stand-up comedian

Don't forget to swing hard, in case you hit the ball.
  Woodie Held, shortstop/outfielder

All I'm asking for is what I want.
    Rickey Henderson, left fielder

I don't know. I never smoked Astroturf.
    Tug McGraw, pitcher, when asked if he preferred grass or
    Astroturf, April 1974

Garry Maddox has turned his life around. He used to be depressed and miserable. Now he's miserable and depressed.
    Harry Kalas, sportscaster and 'Voice of the Phillies', of
    Philadelphia outfielder/center fielder

It's permanent, for now.
    Roberto Kelly, Panamanian player and coach

Two-thirds of the earth is covered by water, the other third is covered by Garry Maddox.
    Ralph Kiner, player and New York Mets announcer, of
    Philadelphia outfielder

Half of Jeff King's extra-base hits last year were extra-base hits.
    Ralph Kiner

The reason the Mets have played so well at Shea this year is they have the best home record in baseball.
    Ralph Kiner

Chuck Hiller was a helluva hitter, but he had iron hands. You couldn't play him on rainy days; his hands would rust.
    Ed Kranepool, first base with New York Mets

You can be stupid once, but idiotic to do it again. I'll settle for being stupid.

> Tony La Russa, St Louis Cardinals manager, refusing
> to make any more predictions that his team would
> win the title

If Mike Scioscia raced his pregnant wife he'd finish third.

> Tommy Lasorda

There goes Rick Monday. He and Manny Mota are so old they were waiters at *The Last Supper*.

> Tommy Lasorda

The average age of our bench is deceased.

> Tommy Lasorda, on veterans Vic Davalillo and
> Manny Mota

The secret to keeping winning streaks is to maximise the victories while at the same time minimising the defeats.

> John Lowenstein, outfielder and sportscaster

It's not that he's a bad outfielder. He just has trouble judging the ball and picking it up.

> Billy Martin, second baseman and manager

The only difference between the Mets and the *Titanic* is that the Mets have a better organist.

> Jim Murray

When I was a little boy, I wanted to be a baseball player and join the circus. With the Yankees, I've accomplished both.

> Graig Nettles

The club didn't mind the added weight, but it gave him two weeks to get down to his playing height.

> Scott Ostler, sports columnist, after Ken Griffey Jr turned up for pre-season training twenty pounds heavier and two inches taller

The last time I smiled so much was for a jury.

> Pascual Pérez, pitcher, after a run of success

He's the world's quietest person. The night he broke Lou Gehrig's record, he went out and painted the town beige.

> Billy Ripken, infielder and broadcaster, on his brother Cal

Therapy can be a good thing. It can be therapeutic.

> Alex Rodriguez, New York Yankees third baseman

How can anyone as slow as you pull a muscle?

> Pete Rose, player and manager, to Tony Pérez, Cuban-born player and manager

If you slid into bases head first for twenty years, you'd be ugly too!

> Pete Rose

I only had one superstition. I made sure to touch all the bases when I hit a home run.

> Babe Ruth, Major League Baseball hitter and home run record holder

We were given a choice. We could either run around the field three times or around Tommy Lasorda once.

> Steve Sax, Major League Baseball right-handed batter

Anything that goes that far ought to have a stewardess on it.
   Paul Splittorff, pitcher for Kansas City Royals, on a George
   Brett home run

I'm not a win-at-all-costs guy. Winning isn't everything. It's second to breathing.
   George Steinbrenner

I am the most loyal player money can buy.
   Don Sutton, pitcher and sportscaster

As a teenager, Gonzo [Luis Gonzalez] was so skinny he had to take steroids just to be on the chess team.
   Greg Swindell, left-handed pitcher and coach

Toronto pitcher David Wells was so disgusted with the *Sports Illustrated* cover depicting him as a big fat slob that he ate the first 50,000 copies.
   Anon.

I call my hairstyle the 'Watergate'. I cover up everything I can.
   Joe Torre

The last time the Chicago Cubs won a World Series was in 1908. The last time they were in one was 1945. Hey, any team can have a bad century.
   Tom Trebelhorn, manager of Milwaukee Brewers and
   Chicago Cubs

Nick Etten's glove fields better with Nick Etten out of it.
   Joe Trimble, writer on baseball, on first baseman for
   Phillies and New York Yankees

What have they lost, nine of their last eight?
    Ted Turner, owner of Atlanta braves

I see three baseballs, but I only swing at the middle one.
    Paul Waner, right fielder, on the perils of drinking

Baseball, it is said, is only a game. True. And the Grand
Canyon is only a hole in Arizona.
    George Will, *Men at Work: The Craft of Baseball*, 1990

Why did I get married in a ballpark? My wife wanted a big
diamond.
    Mookie Wilson, player for New York Mets and Toronto
    Blue Jays

It went quickly, but it was like an eternity.
    Dave Winfield, broadcaster and former player

Baseball statistics are like a girl in a bikini. They show a lot,
but not everything.
    Toby Harrah, Texas Rangers shortstop

Baseball fans love numbers. They love to swirl them around
their mouths like Bordeaux wine.
    Pat Conroy, sportswriter

Baseball games are like snowflakes and fingerprints, no two
are ever alike.
    W. P. Kinsella, Canadian novelist and baseball writer

There have been only two geniuses in the world: Willie
Mays and Willie Shakespeare.
> Tallulah Bankhead, actress, of legendary New York
> and San Francisco Giants center fielder and celebrated
> Stratford-upon-Avon playwright

The great thing about baseball is that there's a crisis
every day.
> Gabe Paul, president New York Yankees

I know a man who is a diamond cutter. He mows the lawn
at Yankee Stadium.
> Anon.

Any time you think you have the game conquered the game
will turn around and punch you right in the nose.
> Mike Schmidt, third baseman Philadelphia Phillies

Baseball is the only game left for people. To play basketball,
you have to be 7 feet 6 inches. To play football, you have to
be the same width.
> Bill Veeck

Hitting is timing. Pitching is upsetting timing.
> Warren Spahn, left-handed pitcher

Baseball and cricket are beautiful and highly stylized mediaeval war substitutes, chess made flesh, a mixture of proud
chivalry and base – in both senses – greed.
> John Fowles, author

A baseball game is twice as much fun if you're seeing it on the company's time.
> William C. Feather, wit

The ball was coming in like a Lear jet.
> T. Glen Coughlin, novelist

Trying to hit Phil Niekro was like trying to eat Jell-O with chopsticks.
> Bobby Murcer, outfielder and sportscaster on pitcher and 'knuckleball' expert

It actually giggles at you as it goes by.
> Rick Monday, on Phil Niekro's knuckleball, quoted in *Sports Illustrated*, 1983

There are two theories on hitting the knuckleball. Unfortunately, neither of them work.
> Charlie Lau, Major League Baseball catcher and coach

The best way to catch a knuckleball is to wait until the ball stops rolling and then pick it up.
> Bob Uecker

[A knuckleball is] a curve ball that doesn't give a damn.
> Jimmy Cannon

I have never willingly chased a ball.
> Robert Morley, actor and wit

I have observed that baseball is not unlike war and, when you get right down to it, we batters are the heavy artillery.
> Ty Cobb, American Major League Baseball catcher and coach

All requests for leave of absence on account of grandmother's funeral, sore throat, housecleaning, lame back, turning off the ringer, headaches, brain storm, cousin's wedding, general ailments or other legitimate excuses must be made out and handed to the boss not later than 10 a.m. on the morning of the game.

Traditional joke notice hung in offices and factories at a
time when all games were played during daylight hours

Baseball fans are junkies, and their heroin is the statistic.

Robert S. Wieder, author

Baseball is drama with an endless run and an everchanging cast.

Joe Garagiola, *Baseball is a Funny Game*, 1960

Hating the New York Yankees is as American as apple pie, unwed mothers and cheating on your income tax.

Mike Royko

I believe in the Church of Baseball. I tried all the major religions and most of the minor ones. I've worshipped Buddha, Allah, Brahma, Vishnu, Shiva, trees, mushrooms and Isadora Duncan. I know things. For instance, there are 108 beads in a Catholic rosary and there are 108 stitches in a baseball. When I learned that, I gave Jesus a chance.

Ron Shelton, *Bull Durham*, 1988

There are no prizes for winning the first half.

Steve Rogers, sportswriter

Babe Ruth wasn't born, the son of a bitch fell from a tree.
Joe Dugan, New York Yankees hitter

I have discovered in twenty years of moving around a ball-park, that the knowledge of the game is usually in inverse proportion to the price of the seats.
Bill Veeck

One of the chief duties of the fan is to engage in arguments with the man behind him. This department of the game has been allowed to run down fearfully.
Robert Benchley, wit

[Orel] Hershiser is the only Major League player to have two consecutive pronouns in his surname.
Roger Ansell, sportswriter

Pitchers, like poets, are born not made.
Cy Young, American Major League Baseball pitcher

Putting lights in Wrigley Field is like putting aluminum siding on the Sistine Chapel.
Roger Simon, political columnist, on the homepark of the Chicago Cubs

Things could be worse. Suppose your errors were counted and published every day, like those of a baseball player.
Anon.

It is an old baseball joke that big-inning baseball is affirmed in the Bible, in Genesis. 'In the big-inning, God created...'
George F. Will, *The Craft of Baseball*, 1990

Lance Armstrong could be pegged as the biggest cheater in sports because of a new report that shows he might have run the most sophisticated doping program in sports history. When news of this got out, Major League Baseball was like, 'Well, we had a good run.'
Late Night with Jimmy Fallon, 2012

Why marry a ballplayer when you can have the whole team?
Mae West, actress, on the Monroe–DiMaggio marriage.

Yogi Berra – Catcher, Fielder And Manager With New York Yankees

No, I'm not superstitious. I'm afraid it would bring me bad luck.

I would like to thank everybody who made this night necessary.
On 'Yogi Berra Night'

If people don't want to come out to the ballpark, nobody's going to stop them.

It ain't like football. You can't make up no-trick plays.

I couldn't have done half of it without the players.
On his achievements.

I never blame myself when I'm not hitting. I just blame the bat, and if it keeps up, I change bats. After all, if I know it isn't my fault that I'm not hitting, how can I get mad at myself?

Little League baseball is a good thing 'cause it keeps the parents off the streets, and it keeps the kids out of the house!

The other team could make trouble for us if they win.

You have to give 100 per cent in the first half of the game. If that isn't enough, in the second half, you have to give what's left.

You can observe a lot just by watching.

Reporter: What would you do if you found a million dollars?
Yogi Berra: If the guy was poor, I would give it back.

Who says I have no standards? 'Course I have standards! They may be very low but at least I have them.

I don't know if it's good for baseball, but it sure beats the hell out of rooming with Phil Rizzuto.
  On the marriage of Yankee Joe DiMaggio and Marilyn
  Monroe

Casey Stengel – Outfielder and Manager of New York Yankees, 1949–60 (nicknamed 'The Old Perfessor')

I got a kid, Greg Goossen, he's nineteen years old and in ten years he's got a chance to be twenty-nine.

This has been a team effort. No one or two guys could have done all this.
  After the Mets lost 120 games in a season

The secret of managing is to keep the guys who hate you away from the guys who are undecided.

They're very much alike in a lot of similarities.

Being with a woman all night never hurt no professional baseball player. It's staying up all night looking for a woman that does him in.

A lot of people my age are dead at the present time.

Ability is the art of getting credit for all the home runs somebody else hits.

All right everyone, line up alphabetically according to your height.

Been in this game 100 years, but I see new ways to lose 'em I never knew existed before.

Don't cut my throat, I may want to do that later myself.

Don't drink in the hotel bar, that's where I do my drinking.

Finding good players is easy. Getting them to play as a team is another story.

Good pitching will always stop good hitting and vice versa.

I came in here and a fella asked me to have a drink. I said I don't drink. Then another fella said, 'Hear you and Joe DiMaggio aren't speaking?', and I said I'll take that drink.

I don't know if he throws a spitball but he sure spits on the ball.

I don't like them fellas who drive in two runs and let in three.

I feel greatly honored to have a ballpark named after me, especially since I've been thrown out of so many.

I got players with bad watches – they can't tell midnight from noon.

I was not successful as a ballplayer, as it was a game of skill.

I was such a dangerous hitter I even got intentional walks during batting practice.

If we're going to win the pennant, we've got to start thinking we're not as good as we think we are.

If you're playing baseball and thinking about managing, you're crazy. You'd be better off thinking about being an owner.

If you're so smart, let's see you get out of the Army.

It's wonderful to meet so many friends that I didn't used to like.

Managing is getting paid for home runs that someone else hits.

Most ballgames are lost, not won.

Never make predictions, especially about the future.

No baseball pitcher would be worth a darn without a catcher who could handle the hot fastball.

Now there's three things you can do in a baseball game: You can win or you can lose or it can rain.

Old-timers, weekends, and airplane landings are alike. If you can walk away from them, they're successful.

Son, we'd like to keep you around this season but we're going to try and win a pennant.

Sure I played, did you think I was born at the age of seventy sitting in a dugout trying to manage guys like you?

The Mets have shown me more ways to lose than I even knew existed.

The team has come along slow but fast.

The trick is growing up without growing old.

The trouble with women umpires is that I couldn't argue with one. I'd put my arms around her and give her a little kiss.

The Yankees don't pay me to win every day, just two out of three.

There comes a time in every man's life, and I've had plenty of them.

They say some of my stars drink whiskey, but I have found that ones who drink milkshakes don't win many ballgames.

They say Yogi Berra is funny. Well, he has a lovely wife and family, a beautiful home, money in the bank, and he plays golf with millionaires. What's funny about that?

They told me my services were no longer desired because they wanted to put in a youth program as an advance way of keeping the club going. I'll never make the mistake of being seventy again.

Two hundred million Americans, and there ain't two good catchers among 'em.

When you are younger you get blamed for crimes you never committed and when you're older you begin to get credit for virtues you never possessed. It evens itself out.

Without losers, where would the winners be?

You got to get twenty-seven outs to win.

You gotta learn that if you don't get it by midnight, chances are you ain't gonna get it, and if you do, it ain't worth it.

You gotta lose 'em some of the time. When you do, lose 'em right.

You have to go broke three times to learn how to make a living.

You have to have a catcher because if you don't you're likely to have a lot of passed balls.

BASEBALL HECKLES

To fielders:
'Does your husband play too?'
'He bought a new glove and forgot to read the instructions.'
'Fetch the ball, boy, fetch! *Good* boy!'
'Get that spring out of your glove!'
'Do you think you'll like this game better when you catch on?'

To pitchers:
'If you'd like, we could move the mound closer!'
'You couldn't hit sand if you fell off a camel!'
'I've seen better pitchers at a Tupperware party!'

To umpires:
'Stevie Wonder could see that one!'
'Do you get any better or is this it?'
'If you're just going to watch the game, buy a ticket!'
'I'm gonna break your cane and shoot your dog!'
'Punch a hole in that mask. You're missing a good game!'
'The optician called ... they'll be ready in thirty minutes.'
'We know you're blind, we've seen your wife!'
'Do you want to use another lifeline?'

To batters:
'Designated What?'
'Betty Crocker makes a better batter than you!'
'This guy couldn't hit a shift key!'
'You're getting less hits than an Amish website!'
  The Baseball Heckle Depot, www.heckledepot.com

GAFFES AND BLOOPERS

Houston has its largest crowd of the night here this evening.
   Jerry Coleman, commentator

The Bible never says anything about dinosaurs. You can't say there were dinosaurs when you never saw them. Somebody actually saw Adam and Eve. No one ever saw a Tyrannosaurus Rex.
   Carl Everett, Major League Baseball outfielder

Who is this babe Ruth and what does she do?
   George Bernard Shaw

Right now I feel that I've got my feet on the ground as far as my head is concerned.
   Bo Belinsky, left-handed pitcher in Major League Baseball

I've never criticised my players in public, and I'll never do it again.
   Bobby Valentine, manager and former player

I was a victim of circumcision.
   Pete Vuckovich, starting pitcher

You don't get your first home run too often.
   Rick Wrona, catcher

You don't want to have to walk back to the dugout with your head between your legs.
   Dmitri Young, outfielder, first baseman and designated hitter

It's a partial sell-out.
  Skip Caray

There is a commotion in the stands. I think it has something to do with a fat lady... I've just been informed that the fat lady is the Queen of Holland.
  Dizzy Dean

Fans – don't fail to miss tomorrow's game.
  Dizzy Dean

Last night's homer was Willie Stargell's 399th home run, leaving him one shy of 500.
  Jerry Coleman

'Hi folks! I'm Gerry Gross...'
  Jerry Coleman, getting his own name wrong

I want all the kids to do what I do, to look up to me. I want all the kids to copulate me.
  Andre Dawson, center fielder and right fielder

The doctors X-rayed my head and found nothing.
  Dizzy Dean

Bruce Sutter has been around for a while, and he's pretty old. He's thirty-five years old. That will give you an idea of how old he is.
  Ron Fairly, player and broadcaster

I watch a lot of baseball on the radio.
  Gerald Ford, American President

I'm a four-wheel-drive pickup type of guy. So is my wife.
    Mike Greenwell, left fielder with Boston Red Sox

Sometimes they [journalists] write what I say and not what I mean.
    Pedro Guerrero, third baseman with Los Angeles Dodgers
    and St Louis Cardinals

This time he grounds it on the ground.
    Ralph Kiner

Some guys are inwardly outgoing.
    Ralph Kiner

The Hall of Fame ceremonies are on the 31st and 32nd of July.
    Ralph Kiner

Tonight, we're honouring one of the all-time greats in baseball, Stan Musial. He's immoral.
    Johnny Logan, Boston Braves shortstop

His reputation preceded him before he got there.
    Don Mattingly, first baseman, coach and manager

Contrary to popular belief, I've always had a wonderful repertoire with my players.
    Danny Ozark

How is our morale? Morality at this point isn't a factor.
    Danny Ozark

Me and George [Steinbrenner] and Billy [Martin] are two of a kind.
    Mickey Rivers, leadoff hitter for New York Yankees

The wind was blowing about 100 degrees.
  Mickey Rivers

I'm not blind to hearing what everyone else hears.
  Zane Smith, Major League left-handed pitcher

David Cone is in a class by himself with three or four
other players.
  George Steinbrenner

BASKETBALL

There are some remarkable parallels between basketball and politics. Michael Jordan has already mastered the skill needed for political success: how to stay aloft without visible means of support.

Margaret Thatcher, British Prime Minister, 1992

Basketball is like photography, if you don't focus, all you have is the negative.

Dan Frisby, wit

Basketball is like war in that offensive weapons are developed first, and it always takes a while for the defense to catch up.

Red Auerbach, coach

Fans never fall asleep at our games, because they're afraid they might get hit by a pass.

George Raveling, coach and commentator

I haven't been able to slam-dunk the basketball for the past five years. Or, for the thirty-eight years before that, either.

Dave Barry, *Miami Herald*

The Atlanta Hawks are a bunch of guys who would prefer to pass kidney stones than pass a basketball.

Bob Weiss, player and coach

The LA Lakers are so good they could run a fast break with a medicine ball.

Rich Donnelly, player and coach

The team is boring and lifeless. For over twenty years the Boston Celtics have stood for something. The only thing they stand for now is the anthem.

Bob Ryan, *Boston Globe*

When I told my wife UConn would win the Big East tournament, she wanted to know why a team from Alaska got into the Big East tournament.

Vic Ziegel, sportswriter and columnist

I was a medium-level juvenile delinquent from Newark who always dreamed about doing a movie. Someone said, 'Hey, here's $7 million, come in and do this genie movie.' What am I going to say, no?

Shaquille O'Neal, former NBA star, 2012

Nothing there but basketball, a game which won't be fit for people until they set the basket umbilicus-high and return the giraffes to the zoo.

Ogden Nash, poet

Some things you just can't question. Like you can't question why two plus two is four. So don't question it, don't try to look it up. I don't know who made it, all I know is it was put in my head that two plus two is four. So certain things happen. Why does it rain? Why am I so sexy? I don't know.

Shaquille O'Neal, player, rapper, analyst

These are my new shoes. They're good shoes. They won't make you rich like me, they won't make you rebound like me, they definitely won't make you handsome like me. They'll only make you have shoes like me. That's it.

Charles Barkley, retired player and analyst

We have a great bunch of outside shooters. Unfortunately, all our games are played indoors.

Weldon Drewe, coach

There are really only two plays: *Romeo and Juliet*, and put the darn ball in the basket.

Abe Lemons, player and coach

I told one player, 'Son, I couldn't understand it with you. Is it ignorance or apathy?' He said, 'Coach, I don't know and I don't care.'

Frank Layden, president, Utah Jazz

Dick Vitale's voice could peel the skin off a potato.

Norman Chad, sportswriter and columnist, of basketball sportscaster

His upper body is built like Mount Olympus. And his lower body is built like Kathie Lee Gifford.

Charles Barkley, of Kevin Willis, retired player

I pay Robey more than anyone to come to my summer basketball camp. The kids can watch him play and see for themselves what not to do.

Larry Bird, legendary player, of retired player Rick Robey

Cotton Fitzsimmons is so short, he's the only coach in the NBA who can sleep in a pillowcase.

    Skip Caray

I call Los Angeles the city of alternatives. If you don't like mountains, we've got the ocean. If you don't like Knott's Berry farm, we've got Disneyland. If you don't like basketball, we've got the Clippers.

    Arsenio Hall, comedian

Like I told the team at half time, Stevie Wonder, Roy Orbison and Ray Charles could have hit some of those shots – or at least come close. We acted like twelve people who were dropped down from outer space, put uniforms on and played like we had never seen each other before.

    Jim Cleamons, retired player and coach

He has so many fish hooks in his nose, he looks like a piece of bait.

    Bob Costas, of the nose piercings of Dennis Rodman

He doesn't cut that hair, he mows it.

    Chick Hearn, sportscaster, of Dennis Rodman's green hair

The new Dennis Rodman doll is $19.95, assault and battery not included.

    David Letterman, late-night comic

Dennis Rodman's latest hairstyle looks like an inkblot test I get at my psychiatrist.

    Bill Wennington, retired Canadian player

Dennis Rodman plays a villain in the movie *Double Team*. That's like hiring Elizabeth Taylor to play a divorcee.

Tom Powers, actor

When Stanley Roberts was here, we had to remove an obstruction from his throat. It was a pizza.

Pat Williams, motivational speaker, of retired player

Stanley Roberts's idea of a salad is putting a piece of lettuce on a pizza.

Pat Williams

I knew that if he shot off his mouth long enough, he'd get something right.

Billy Tubbs, coach, of sportscaster Dick Vitale

If they can keep his wheelchair greased and his walker handy, he'll do fine.

Dick Motta, coach, of veteran coach Bill Fitch

I learned a long time ago that minor surgery is when they do the operation on someone else, not you.

Bill Walton, center-forward and TV sportscaster

I've been here so long that when I got here the Dead Sea wasn't even sick.

Wimp Sanderson, on his 916th game as coach at the
University of Alabama

I'll always remember this as the night Michael and I combined to score 70 points.

Stacey King, NBA center, after Michael Jordan had scored
a play-off record 69 points

In my prime I could have handled Michael Jordan. Of course, he would be only twelve years old.

Jerry Sloan, NBA player and head coach

I sight down my nose to shoot, and now my nose isn't straight since I broke it. That's why my shooting has been off.

Barrie Haynie, Centenary College player, on his jump shot

The way to stop Kareem Abdul-Jabbar is to get real close to him and breathe on his goggles.

John Kerr, player, coach and color commentator

The way defenses are operating these days, the other team starts picking you up when you walk out of the hotel lobby.

Doc Hayes, head basketball coach at Southern Methodist University

If you've got 10,000 people seated in an arena and everybody's standing up and hollering and you expect the coaches and players to be quiet and relaxed, you're going to have to give them a sedative. Then the coach probably will be fired at the end of the season and the players cut off their scholarships.

Doc Hayes, reacting to the suggestion that coaches must remain seated during the game

We told Stanley Roberts to go on a water diet, and Lake Superior disappeared.

Pat Williams, Orlando Magic general manager

To say a good defensive center is more important than a high-scoring forward is like saying that the intestinal tract is more vital than the circulatory system.

Tetford Taylor

In basketball, the first person to touch the ball shoots it. Either that or the coach carefully diagrams a set play and then the first player to touch it shoots it.

Gene Klein, founding partner of Seattle SuperSonics

Tracy McGrady is doing things we've never seen from anybody – from any planet!

Bill Walton, of shooting guard McGrady now with
Qingdao Eagles

The way my team are doing, we could get Wilt Chamberlain in a trade and find out that he's really two midgets Scotch-taped together.

Gene Shue, player and coach in the National Basketball Association

Giving 'Magic' the basketball is like giving Hitler an army, Jesse James a gang, or Genghis Khan a horse. Devastation. Havoc.

Jim Murray, *Los Angeles Times* sportswriter, of Magic Johnson

Shooting is just like toenails. They may fall off occasionally, but you know they'll always come back.

Charles Johnson, player for Golden State Warriors

If you can walk with your head in the clouds and keep your feet on the ground, you can make a million dollars in the NBA.

Gary Dornhoefer, Philadelphia Flyers ice hockey player

Basketball has so much showboating you'd think it was invented by Jerome Kern.

Art Spander, sportswriter

I knew I was dog meat. Luckily, I'm the high-priced dog meat that everybody wants. I'm the good-quality dog meat. I'm the Alpo of the NBA.

Shaquille O'Neal

Magic Johnson is the best player who plays on the ground, and Michael Jordan is the best player who plays in the air.

John Paxson, point guard and administrator

They say that nobody is perfect. Then they tell you practice makes perfect. I wish they'd make up their minds.

Wilt Chamberlain, legendary player

Part of the charm of basketball lies in the fact that it's a simple game to understand. Players race up and down a fairly small area indoors and stuff the ball into a ring with Madonna's dress hanging on it.

Dan Jenkins, author and sportswriter

We can't win at home. We can't win on the road. As general manager, I just can't figure out where else to play.

Pat Williams, on his team's 7–27 record in 1992

Eliminate the referees, raise the basket 4 feet, double the size of the basketball, limit the height of the players to 5 feet 9 inches, bring back the centre jump, allow taxi drivers in for free and allow the players to carry guns.

Ali McGuire, head coach and Basketball Hall of Famer, on how to make the game more exciting

The only way I can make five A's is when I sign my name.

Alaa Adbehuby, Egyptian-American power forward, on his academic record

This is the second most exciting indoor sport, and the other one shouldn't have spectators.

Dick Vertlieb, basketball administrator

What is so fascinating about sitting around watching a bunch of pituitary cases stuff a ball through a hoop?

Woody Allen, *Annie Hall,* 1977

When it's played the way is spozed to be played, basketball happens in the air; flying, floating, elevated above the floor, levitating the way oppressed peoples of this earth imagine themselves in their dreams.

John Edgar Wideman, basketball player, writer and academic

The secret is to have eight great players and four others who will cheer like crazy.

Jerry Tarkanian, coach

GAFFES AND BLOOPERS

Any time Detroit scores more than 100 points and holds the other team below 100 points, they almost always win.

Doug Collins, basketball player and coach

Left hand, right hand, it doesn't matter. I'm amphibious.

Charles Shackleford, player with New Jersey Nets

BEACH VOLLEYBALL

As I write these words there are semi-naked women playing beach volleyball in the middle of the Horse Guards Parade immortalised by Canaletto. They are glistening like wet otters and the water is plashing off the brims of the spectators' sou'westers. The whole thing is magnificent and bonkers.

Boris Johnson, mayor of London, describing the Olympic beach volleyball, 2012

A mere forty years ago, beach volleyball was just beginning. No bureaucrat would have invented it, and that's what freedom is all about.

Newt Gingrich, Republican politician

I bust mine so I can kick yours.

T-shirt slogan

Some call them opponents...
We call them victims!

T-shirt slogan

Tossed and turned all night,
Slept through the alarm,
Was late for school,
Completely spaced the test,
Broke up with my boyfriend,
Played volleyball...
Not a bad day.
    Poster

Most people think that volleyball is twenty-two people on the beach who quit playing when the hamburgers are ready.
    Steve Timmons, double Olympic gold medallist

BILLIARDS

Q: What do you find on a billiards table that you also find in men's trousers?
A: Pockets!
 Anon.

Proficiency at billiards is proof of a misspent youth.
 Herbert Spencer, philosopher

It is impossible to imagine Goethe or Beethoven being good at billiards or golf.
 H. L. Mencken, wit

BOWLS

If only Hitler and Mussolini could have a good game of
bowls once a week at Geneva, I feel that Europe would not
be as troubled as it is.

R. G. Briscow, British politician, during the
Second World War

There is plenty of time to win this game, and to thrash the
Spaniards too.

Sir Francis Drake, 1587, attrib.

See also TENPIN BOWLING

BOXING

The hardest thing about prize-fighting is picking up your teeth with a boxing glove on.
  Kin Hubbard, wit

To me, boxing is like a ballet, except there's no music, no choreography, and the dancers hit each other.
  Jack Handey, wit

After the fight I was presented with a special cup – to keep my teeth in.
  Anon.

I had quite a good record in the ring. I fought a hundred fights and won all but ninety-nine of them!
  Anon.

I quit school in the sixth grade because of pneumonia. Not because I had it, but because I couldn't spell it.
  Rocky Graziano, welterweight boxer

Carl's the kind of guy where if you played in a football friendly, he'd get sent off for a tackle after five minutes.
  Steve Bunce, pundit and columnist, of Carl Froch,
  English boxer

You are an embarrassment to boxing. I am going to slap you like a little girl.

Miguel Cotto, Puerto Rican boxer to his opponent,
Mexican-American Antonio Margarito

The boxer struggled to his corner and, gasping for breath, asked his second, 'What round is this?'

And the second said, 'As soon as the bell rings, it'll be the first.'

Anon.

If you ever get belted and see three fighters through a haze, go after the one in the middle. That's what ruined me – I went after the two guys on the end.

Max Baer, world heavyweight champion, 1934–5

I am not overly scared by comments from someone whose biggest hit to date has been a YouTube video where he punches himself in the face.

Alexander Povetkin, Russian boxer, of Anglo-Irish
opponent Tyson Fury

They say I cannot punch, but you should see me putting the cat out at night.

Chris Finnegan, light-heavyweight boxer

Lennox Lewis, I'm coming for you man. My style is impetuous. My defense is impregnable, and I'm just ferocious. I want your heart. I want to eat his children. Praise be to Allah!

Mike Tyson, heavyweight champion

The champion, Jess Willard, had about as much chance in this fight as a dish-faced chimpanzee in a beauty contest.
   Arthur 'Bugs' Baer, New York journalist and humorist, on
   Jack Dempsey winning the world heavyweight title

Don Cockell is the biggest thing on canvas since 'The Wreck of the Hesperus'.
   Anon. on the British heavyweight

If Larry Holmes is the people's champion, then asparagus is the people's vegetable.
   Bernie Lincicome, *Chicago Tribune*

In his prime, Joe Bugner had the physique of a Greek statue but he had fewer moves.
   Hugh McIlvanney, British sportswriter

I've been knocked down more than any heavyweight champion in history, but I consider that a compliment, because I must have got up more than any heavyweight champion.
   Floyd Patterson, heavyweight champion

Mexicans are always tough with lots of heart; Koreans raw and gritty; the poor British tend to stand up straight and take it on the chops, bleeding almost before the opening bell.
   Stephen Brunt, sportswriter

Sleep came as it must come to all British heavyweights, midway in the fifth round.
   'Red' Smith, sportswriter, on Bruce Woodcock

I was the only fighter in Cleveland who wore a rearview mirror.
　　Bob Hope, quoted in *Bob Hope: Portrait of a Superstar*, 1981

First your legs go. Then you lose your reflexes. Then you lose your friends.
　　Willie Pep, world featherweight champion

In boxing the right cross-counter is distinctly one of those things it is more blessed to give than to receive.
　　P. G. Wodehouse, *The Pothunters*, 1902

I'll never forget my first fight ... all of a sudden I found someone I knew in the fourth row. It was me. He hit me amongst my nose.
　　Henny Youngman, 1940

It's gonna be a thrilla, a chilla and a killa, when I get the gorilla in Manila.
　　Muhammad Ali, legendary heavyweight champion, before
　　his fight with Joe Frazier in the Philippines, 1975

Nothing is going to stop Tyson that doesn't have a motor attached.
　　David Brenner, *New York Times*, 1988

Now, to be a successful boxer, it is said, one must always consider the rights of others.
　　Professor Ned Donnelly, *Self Defence or The Art of
　　Boxing*, 1879

In the first round I had the champ down on one knee.
He was bending over to see if I was still breathing!
Anon.

His trainer called him 'Laundry'. He was always hanging
over the ropes!
Anon.

I can lick any man with one hand! Unfortunately, my opponent had two.
Anon.

I never see my husband at breakfast. Being a boxer, he never
gets up before the stroke of ten.
Anon.

I used to be a boxer. I fought Joe Frazier once. In the first
round, I really had him worried.
He thought he'd killed me.
Anon.

I used to run five miles before every fight, but my opponents
always managed to catch me and beat me up anyway.
Anon.

I would have won my last fight if the referee hadn't stood
on my hand.
Anon.

I wouldn't say he's very confident of winning this fight. He's already sold the advertising space on the soles of his shoes.
Anon.

I'll say this for my opponent: he was a clean fighter. You could tell by the way he kept wiping the floor with me.
Anon.

I'm very superstitious. I keep a horseshoe in my glove for luck!
Anon.

Just before the fight started, my trainer started yelling in my ear. He told me that my opponent beat his wife, kicked his kids and starved his mother. That really made me fighting mad. If there's one thing I can't stand, it's someone shouting in my ear!
Anon.

Manager: You can beat him hands down!
Boxer: But he doesn't want to keep his hands down!
Anon.

There was an old boxer who was having trouble sleeping. So the doctor told him, 'Just lie down, relax and start counting to 1,000.'
A week later the boxer came back to the surgery. He said, 'It's no good. I keep jumping up at the count of nine!'
Anon.

There was one thing he never got to see in the course of his boxing career – the end of the first round.
Anon.

He's gonna need an industrial-strength toothpick to pick the leather out of his teeth. I'm gonna hit this man so hard he's gonna grow an Afro.

Michael Olajide, middleweight, before fighting Iran Barkley

When you're knocked down with a good shot, you don't feel pain. In fact it's a very lovable feeling. Maybe it's like taking dope. It's like floating. You feel you love everybody – like a hippie, I guess.

Floyd Patterson

My best punch was a rabbit punch.
Trouble was, they wouldn't let me fight rabbits.

Anon.

On taking a punch to the head – it opens a spacious firmament to the bewildered eyes, wherein you discover more planets in a second than most distinguished astronomers observe in a lifetime.

Professor Ned Donnelly, *Self Defence or The Art of Boxing*, 1879

What a fight! I came out of my corner and I tried a right, then a left jab, then another left jab, then a right uppercut. And then my opponent came out of *his* corner.

Anon.

When I was a boxer, they used to call me Rembrandt. I was always on the canvas!

Anon.

Earnie Shavers hit me, man, and knocked me face down on the canvas. I was in the land of make-believe. I heard saxophones, trombones. I saw little blue rats, and they were all smoking cigars and drinking whisky.

James 'Quick' Tillis, heavyweight

Jack Dempsey hit me hardest, 'cos Dempsey hit me 211,000 dollars' worth, while Joe Louis only hit me 36,000 dollars' worth.

Jack Sharkey, heavyweight, on measuring punches in terms of prize money

The bell went ding and I went dong.

Lloyd Honeyghan, British welterweight, on hitting Johnny Bumphus while he was still rising from his stool

I don't know, I've never hit myself.

Elisha Obed, Bahamian middleweight, on being asked to name his best punch

Jack Dempsey hits like an epileptic pile-driver.

Harry C. Witwer, commentator

George Chuvalo's best punch is a left cheek to the right glove.

Larry Merchant, writer

The bum was up and down so many times I thought he was an Otis elevator.

Harry Kabakoff, trainer and manager, after another loss by Chango Cruz, Mexican featherweight

Boxing is built on bums. How else are you gonna know good from bad? How else is a good boy gonna get on top and get experience unless he fights bums? I tell ya, there's a shortage of bums.

  Al Braverman, boxer, manager and trainer

Héctor Camacho's great dream is to die in his own arms.

  Irving Rudd, sports publicist, of Puerto Rican lightweight

I was once knocked out by a Mexican bantamweight – six of my pals were swinging him around by his heels at the time.

  Randall 'Tex' Cobb, boxer-turned-actor

Herol Graham has turned defensive boxing into a poetic art. Trouble is, nobody ever got knocked out by a poem.

  Eddie Shaw, Irish coach

I'd love to fight Gerry Cooney. But I have my price – twenty-five cents and a loose woman.

  Randall 'Tex' Cobb

Me and Jake LaMotta grew up in the same neighbourhood. You wanna know how popular Jake was? When we played hide and seek, nobody ever looked for LaMotta.

  Rocky Graziano

If a boxer ever went as crazy as Nijinsky, all the wowsers in the world would be screaming 'punch drunk!' Well, who hit Nijinsky? And why isn't there a campaign against ballet? It gives girls thick legs.

  A. J. Liebling, *The Sweet Science* , 1956

It's marvellous. You win the championship of the world and the first thing they say to you is 'Piss off!'

Jim Watt, world champion lightweight, on being asked for a
drug test urine sample immediately after winning a world title

Brian London possesses the most unbeautiful face – it looks as if it, at one time, fell apart and was reassembled by a drunken mechanic.

Michael Parkinson, British sportswriter of British
heavyweight

Bob Arum is one of the worst people in the western hemisphere. I don't know the eastern hemisphere very well, but I suspect he'd be one of the worst people there too, if he went.

Cus D'Amato, trainer and manager on boxing promoter

Because this is a title fight, I can have four people in the corner and I'll have an extra cut-man. I'll also have an extra stool, one for Vinny to sit on, and the other to throw at him if he doesn't listen to me.

Lou Duva, trainer and manager, on Vinny Paz fighting
Greg Haugen

You can sum up this sport in two words: you never know.

Lou Duva

I can close any cut in the world in fifty seconds, so long as it ain't a total beheading.

Adolph Ritacco, on his prowess as a cut-man

I've made the national anthem a six-point underdog.

Jimmy 'The Greek' Snyder, commentator and bookmaker,
on Joe Frazier's attempt to sing 'The Star Spangled Banner'
in tune

Since I've retired, I eat less, weigh less, train less and care less.
  Ray Mancini, lightweight champion

His legs turned to spaghetti and I was all over him like the sauce.
  Vinny Paz, Italian-American lightweight, on hitting a
  shaken opponent

Boxing is a great exercise ... as long as you can yell 'cut' whenever you want to.
  Sylvester Stallone, actor

Saying that Howard Cosell quit commentating on boxing because it's sleazy is like saying Nixon quit politics because it's crooked.
  Paul Gereffi, boxing writer

To hell with the Queen of Marksbury!
  Pierre Bouchard, Canadian hockey player

I was 6 foot 1 inch when I started fighting, but with all the uppercuts I'm up to 6 foot 5 inches.
  Chuck Wepner, heavyweight

My girlfriend boos when we make love because she knows it turns me on.
  Héctor Camacho, Puerto Rican lightweight

I see two fellows in the ring. I hit the one that isn't there and the one that is there hits me.
  Anonymous boxer

INDIVIDUAL BOXERS

Muhammad Ali (Cassius Clay)

It's hard to be humble when you're as great as I am.
Muhammad Ali

It's just a job. Grass grows, birds fly, waves pound the shore.
I beat people up.
Muhammad Ali

I can be found the next couple of months trying to perfect
my new punch – the lip-buttoner.
Archie Moore, before his fight with Cassius Clay

When he got in trouble in the ring, [Ali] imagined a door
swung open and inside he could see neon, orange, and green
lights blinking, and bats blowing trumpets and alligators
blowing trombones, and he could hear snakes screaming.
Weird masks and actors' clothes hung on the wall, and if he
stepped across the sill and reached for them, he knew that
he was committing himself to destruction.
George Plympton, American sports journalist

I'm so fast I could hit you before God gets the news.
Muhammad Ali

I'll beat Floyd Patterson so bad, he'll need a shoehorn to
put his hat on.
Muhammad Ali

I'd like to borrow Ali's body for forty-eight hours. There are three guys I'd like to beat up and four women I'd like to make love to.

Jim Murray, reporter for the *Los Angeles Times*

Muhammad Ali wouldn't have hit Joe Louis on the bum with a handful of rice.

Tommy Farr, Welsh heavyweight

Don't watch Ali's gloves, arms or legs when he's fighting. Watch his brain.

José Torres, light-heavyweight champion

Muhammad Ali was so quick he would click off the light and be in bed before the room got dark.

George Foreman, heavyweight champion

Muhammad Ali isn't a puncher. He just hit me so many times I didn't know where I was.

Brian London, British opponent

At home I am a nice guy, but I don't want the world to know. Humble people, I've found, don't get very far.

Muhammad Ali

When it comes to ballyhoo, Muhammad Ali made Barnum and Bailey look like non-starters, and he had the incandescent quality of the real star which would have made him famous, even if his gift was knitting not fighting.

Michael Parkinson

My toughest fight was with my first wife. And she won every round.

Muhammad Ali

Why should I feel sorry for Ali? He got two-and-a-half million dollars for being beaten up. Most of us in this city have to pay for the privilege.

Anon., after Ali had been beaten by Joe Frazier in New York

Butch Lewis is making no attempt to get out of the corner ... and is hanging his chin out like a lantern in a storm.

Reg Gutteridge, British commentator, during a fight against Muhammad Ali

Float like a butterfly, sting like a bee.

Muhammad Ali

He stings like a bee, but lives like a W.A.S.P.

Eamonn Andrews, British TV host, on Ali's changed lifestyle.

Ali fell over the ropes as if he was leaning backwards out of the bathroom window to see if the cat was on the roof.

George Plimpton, sportswriter, on Ali's rope-a-dope tactics against George Foreman

He now floats like an anchor, stings like a moth.

Ray Gandolf, sportswriter, on Ali, still fighting at thirty-nine

Frank Bruno

Frank Bruno has a chin of such pure Waterford crystal, it gives rise to the old adage that people who live in glass jaws shouldn't throw punches. The biggest danger in fighting Bruno is that you might get hit by flying glass.

Jim Murray, before the Mike Tyson rematch

Frank Bruno says I'm chicken. Well you can tell him I've
come home to roost.
    Joe Bugner, British heavyweight

By the way Frank Bruno went on about beating Bugner,
you'd have thought he had won the Booker prize, not just
taken time to out-jab an old man bullocking around pretty
harmlessly in the pension queue.
    Frank Keating, *The Guardian*

If Bruno insists on calling himself a world champion, then
he is champion only of that portion of the globe not inhab-
ited by any number of superior heavyweights including
Riddick Bowe, Mike Tyson, Evander Holyfield, Lennox
Lewis, Bruce Seldon, George Foreman, Luciano Pavarotti,
Keith Chegwin, Mr Eric Younghusband, 22 Bramble Lane,
Stoke Poges...
    Robert Philip, *Daily Telegraph*

Joe Bugner fought Bruno like the objective of boxing was
to get hit on the jaw.
    Jim Jacobs, boxing film collector

Frank Bruno's fall was that of a felled oak. As the dust
settled there was a silence, and then followed the gentle
rustle of falling leaves of greenbacks.
    Frank Keating, *Punch*

Frank Bruno – boxing's loss was pantomime's gain.
    Anon.

After all the years of punishment you've taken, you must be
thinking about giving up pantomime.
    Clive Anderson, TV host, to Frank Bruno

It was like a Michael Jackson concert, Pavarotti, Vera Lynn and VE-Day all rolled into one.

> Frank Bruno, on winning the world title, *Sportsnight*, BBC TV, 1995

George Foreman

There seems only one way to beat George Foreman: shell him for three days and then send the infantry in.

> Hugh McIlvanney

Sure the fight was fixed. I fixed it with my right hand.

> George Foreman, after knocking out Michael Moorer

He's got a nutritionist, and I've got room service.

> George Foreman, on Evander Holyfield's dietary needs

I've seen George Foreman shadow boxing. And the shadow won.

> Muhammad Ali

Marvin Hagler

If they cut my bald head open, they will find one big boxing glove. That's all I am.

> Marvin Hagler

It's hard to get up at six o'clock every morning when you're wearing silk pyjamas.

> Marvin Hagler, on the problems of success

Sugar Ray Leonard

Sugar Ray Leonard's retirements last about as long as Elizabeth Taylor's marriages.
   Bob Arum, boxing promoter

Johnny Carson: When do the wounds from the fight heal?
Sugar Ray Leonard: When the check clears.
   TV host to Sugar Ray Leonard

We've all been blessed with God-given talents. Mine just happens to be beating people up.
   Sugar Ray Leonard

Sonny Liston

The only thing my old man ever gave me was a beating.
   Sonny Liston, heavyweight boxer

Don't matter where the fight is. My punches are just as hard in Chicago as in New York.
   Sonny Liston, on his fight with Floyd Patterson being
   switched to the Windy City

It don't matter as long as he can count up to ten.
   Sonny Liston, on choosing a referee for his fight against
   Floyd Patterson

A boxing match is like a cowboy movie. There's gotta be good guys and there's gotta be bad guys. And that's what people pay for – to see the bad guys get beat.
   Sonny Liston

Joe Louis

It was said that if all the fighters who lost to Joe Louis were laid end to end ... we wouldn't be a bit surprised.
Anon.

Everyone has a plan until they've been hit.
Joe Louis

It is like someone jammed an electric light bulb in your face and busted it. I thought half my head was blowed off. When he knocked me down, I could have stayed there for three weeks.
Jim Braddock, on being hit by Joe Louis

I only have to read Joe Louis's name and my nose starts to bleed again.
Tommy Farr

Rocky Marciano

Rocky Marciano didn't know enough boxing to know what a feint was. He never tried to out-guess you. He just kept trying to knock your brains out.
Archie Moore, light-heavyweight world champion

Rocky Marciano couldn't carry my jockstrap.
Larry Holmes

Sugar Ray Robinson

I fought Sugar Ray Robinson so many times that I'm lucky I didn't get diabetes.

  Jake LaMotta

You always say, 'I'll quit when I start to slide.' Then, one morning, you wake up and you've slid.

  Sugar Ray Robinson

Mike Tyson

Tyson fights like you stole something from him or said something nasty about his family.

  Mike Acri, promoter

Mike's like a Gershwin or Beethoven. You go for the quality of the performance, not the longevity of it.

  Don King, promoter, on the brevity of Mike Tyson's
  early fights

Mike Tyson dropped me and when I looked up, the count was on five. I said to myself, 'Damn, whatever happened to one to four.'

  Buster Mathis Jr, after being knocked out

Everything Tyson's got has 'goodnight' written on it.

  Mills Lane, referee

Mike Tyson's not all that bad. If you dig deep ... dig real deep, dig, dig, dig, dig, dig, deep, deep, go all the way to China ...
I'm sure, you'll find there's a nice guy in there.
George Foreman

When Mike Tyson gets mad, you don't need a referee, you need a priest.
Jim Murray

Frank Bruno figures to be the biggest British disaster since the *Titanic*. Las Vegas will bet you even money Bruno doesn't last the first round. He's 7/1 to lose, 6/1 to get knocked out, he's probably 7/5 to get killed.
Jim Murray, before the first Tyson fight for a year-and-a-half

It's good that Mike Tyson has been granted parole. More steps like this must be taken to make our prisons safer places.
Greg Cote

He's the first guy to drive a $300,000 car with license plates he made himself.
Jay Leno, after Mike Tyson bought four expensive cars on his release from prison

Mike Tyson was a referee at Wrestlemania XIV, and at the end of the night he gave the crowd the finger. The weird part is it was Evander Holyfield's finger.
Conan O'Brien, late-night host

Boxers on Boxers

He doesn't know how to fight, he doesn't know how to stand and he's as wide open as the Holland Tunnel.
    Al Certo on Roy Jones

Some people say George is fit as a fiddle, but I think he looks more like a cello.
    Lou Duva on George Foreman

The fella is a bore. He could be at a party and no one would know he's there. His poster could put people to sleep.
    George Foreman on Buster Douglas

Billy Wells was all chin from the waist up.
    Frank Moran

Tommy Morrison proved that he is an ambidextrous fighter. He can get knocked out with either hand.
    Bert Sugar, boxing writer

He has everything a boxer needs except speed, stamina, a punch and ability to take punishment. In other words he owns a pair of shorts.
    Blackie Sherrod of unnamed contender

Rick Thornberry is a poor bum whose head should be used to keep doors from slamming on a windy day.
    Anthony Mundine

I'm not saying Tommy Hearns is a cheapskate, but he squeezes a nickel so tight, the Indian sits on the buffalo.
    Irving Rudd

Scott Harrison has pissed away a career then acted as if he is the victim. He doesn't have a chip on his shoulder, but a bag of King Edwards.

Frank Warren, promoter

Don King – Promoter

Since then we've changed the locks.

Mayor James McNutty, on Don King's award of the keys to the city of Scranton, Pennsylvania

Don King is one of the great humanitarians of our time. He has risen above that great term, prejudice. He has screwed everybody he has ever been around. Hog, dog, or frog, it don't matter to Don. If you got a quarter, he wants the first 26 cents.

Randall 'Tex' Cobb

One day Don King will asphyxiate by the force of his own exhaust.

Carmen Graciano, trainer

Don King took a ride on a dogsled. It was so cold, he had his hands in his own pockets.

Chris Myers

We all know what Don King is, but if you keep a snake in the room with a light on, you can control him.

Mike Tyson

I tried to stay away from King. You can't do it. It's like staying away from taxes. Sooner or later, he'll get you.

Pinklon Thomas

Don King dresses like a pimp and speechifies like a store-front preacher.

John Schulian, sportswriter

Don King doesn't care about black or white. He just cares about green.

Larry Holmes

Lennox Lewis has two chances of getting a rematch with McCall – no chance and slim. And slim has just left town.

Don King, after Lennox Lewis lost his world title to
Oliver McCall

They went down the list of every known charge conceivable to man: racketeering, skimming, kickback, ticket scalping, fixing fights, pre-ordaining fights, vitiating officials, corrupting judges – all the way down to laundering money. Everything, but the Lindbergh baby.

Don King, on an FBI investigation into his finances

GAFFES AND BLOOPERS

Sure there have been injuries and deaths in boxing – but none of them serious.

Alan Minter, Welsh boxer

It has made the richest prize in sport the richest prize in sport.

Joe Bugner

Harry Carpenter – BBC Commentator

Magri has to do well against the unknown Mexican who comes from a famous family of five boxing brothers.

The question looming over Magri, is not will he keep the title, but can he?

Now it comes to a simple equation – who can stand the heat.

He looks up at him through blood-smeared lips.

Marvellous oriental pace he's got, just like a Buddhist statue.

Pedroza – the crown on his head hanging by a thread.

This boxer doing what's expected of him, bleeding from the nose.

It's not one of Bruno's fastest wins ... but it's one of them.

The Mexicans ... these tiny little men from South America.

They said it would last two rounds – they were half right, it lasted four.

See also: KARATE, MIXED MARTIAL ARTS

CARD GAMES

A Smith and Wesson beats four aces.
  Michael Enright, broadcaster

Trust everybody – but cut the cards.
  Finley Peter Dunne, humorous writer

I say, let's banish bridge. Let's find some pleasant way of being miserable together.
  Don Herold, wit

Cards are war, in disguise of a sport.
  Charles Lamb, 'Mrs Battle's Opinions on Whist', 1823

He caught himself cheating while playing patience – and never spoke to himself again.
  Anon.

A great social success is a pretty girl who plays her cards as carefully as if she were plain.
  F. Scott Fitzgerald, novelist

Let's play a friendly game of cards!
No, let's play bridge!
  Anon.

Fate was kind to him, dealing him a hand of five aces.
  Harry Wilson

One should always play fairly when one has the winning cards.
  Oscar Wilde, playwright

See also: POKER

CHEERLEADING

Repel them. Repel them. Induce them to relinquish the spheroid!
  Indiana University football cheer

It's hard to be humble when you can jump, stunt, and tumble!
  T-shirt slogan

I'm a crowd pleasing, cheer yelling, stunt building, short-skirt wearin', toe touching, hand clapping, big smilin', kick-ass CHEERLEADER!
  T-shirt slogan

It's a cheer thing, you wouldn't understand.
  T-shirt slogan

Cheerleaders are angels – we're the only humans who can fly.
  T-shirt slogan

The Orlando Magic were so bad last season, the cheerleaders stayed home and phoned in their cheers.
  Pat Williams, Orlando Magic general manager

One of the great disappointments of a football game is that the cheerleaders never seem to get injured.

New York Tribune

Cheerleading is more than a sport; it's an attitude.

Anon.

I don't play the field – I rule the sidelines.

T-shirt slogan

WIMPS LIFT WEIGHTS, CHEERLEADERS LIFT PEOPLE

Bumper sticker

Flying is the second best thrill to cheerleaders; being caught is the first.

Anon.

IF CHEERLEADERS ARE SO EASY, WHY AREN'T YOU WITH ONE?

Bumper sticker

The NFL cheerleaders are gorgeous and sexy, but are their cheers helping anybody? Ever see a player interviewed after the game say, 'We were down pretty big in the fourth quarter but then the cheerleaders started chanting, "Defense!" That's when it dawned on the coach, "Them girls are right!"'

Gary Gulman, comedian

WE CHEER SO YOU DON'T HAVE TO!

Bumper sticker

CHEERLEADERS KNOW THAT PYRAMIDS WERE NOT BUILT IN EGYPT

Bumper sticker

Cheerleaders are simply a jump above the rest.
　　Anon.

If cheerleading got any easier, it would be called football.
　　T-shirt slogan

Players: a vital part of any sporting event, they entertain the crowd in the intervals between timeouts so the cheerleaders can take a well-earned break.
　　Anon.

Without a conductor it's only an orchestra; without cheerleaders it's only a game.
　　Anon.

Eat. Sleep. Cheer. Repeat.
　　T-shirt slogan

ANY MAN CAN HOLD A GIRL'S HAND, BUT ONLY THE ELITE CAN HOLD HER FEET!
　　Bumper sticker

PEACE, LOVE, AND CHEERLEADING. THE REST IS JUST DETAILS.
　　Bumper sticker

Just because you don't run across goal-lines, slam dunk basketballs, or hit home runs, doesn't mean you can't change the score!
　　Anon.

Open up the barn door, kick out the hay,
We are the girls from the USA!
Turn on the radio, and what do ya hear?
3LW doin' a cheer,
Fire cracker, Fire cracker, BOOM! BOOM! BOOM!
Fire cracker, Fire cracker, BOOM! BOOM! BOOM!
Boys have got the muscles, coaches got the brains,
Cheerleaders have the pom poms and we win the game!

See also: AMERICAN FOOTBALL, COLLEGE FOOTBALL

CHESS

I was playing chess with my friend and he said, 'Let's make this interesting.'
So we stopped playing chess.
 Matt Kirshen, Edinburgh, 2011

My problem with chess was that all my pieces wanted to end the game as soon as possible.
 Dave Barry, *Miami Herald*

A computer once beat me at chess, but it was no match for me at kickboxing.
 Emo Philips, comedian

I failed to make the chess team because of my height.
 Woody Allen, comedian

I saw a fascinating story in the paper yesterday. There was this seven-year-old girl playing in a chess tournament in Moscow against twenty world-champion chess players – all at the same time.
 And would you believe it – she lost every game!
 Anon.

... most chess games have all the raw-nerved excitement of the home-shopping channel with the sound turned down.
Richard Morrison, *The Times*

I had lunch with a chess champion the other day. I knew he was a chess champion because it took him twenty minutes to pass the salt.
Eric Sykes, actor and comic

Chess is a foolish expedient for making idle people think they are doing something clever when they are only wasting their time.
George Bernard Shaw, playwright

When a man's house is on fire, it's time to break off chess.
Thomas Fuller, clergyman and author, 1732

It is impossible to win gracefully at chess.
No man has yet said 'Mate!' in a voice which failed to sound to his opponent bitter, boastful and malicious.
A. A. Milne, *Not That It Matters*, 1919

Trying to stop [Bobby] Fischer in full flight is like trying to stop a runaway train with a butterfly net.
Liam Fowler

CLIMBING

Mountain climbers rope themselves together to prevent the sensible ones from going home.
  Earl Wilson, columnist

It's always further than it looks.
It's always taller than it looks.
And it's always harder than it looks.
  Anon., *The Three Rules of Mountaineering*

There are only three real sports: bull-fighting, car racing and mountain climbing. All the others are mere games.
  Ernest Hemingway, novelist

Climbing may be hard, but it's easier than growing up.
  Ed Sklar, climber

Some of the world's greatest feats were accomplished by people not smart enough to know they were impossible.
  Doug Lawson, climber

To qualify for mountain rescue work, you have to pass our test. The doctor holds a flashlight to your ear. If he can see light coming out the other one, you qualify.
  Willi Pfisterer, climber and mountain rescue expert

As a member of an escorted tour, you don't even have to know the Matterhorn isn't a tuba.

Temple Fielding, travel writer

No snowflake in an avalanche ever feels responsible.

George Burns, comedian

The law of gravity is strictly enforced.

Sign in Yosemite

As in any alpine region, the weather is changeable, protection questionable, route-finding bewildering, rockfall frequent and descents tedious. In short, it's everything you could ever ask for.

The Canadian Alpine Journal, 1993

I have not had to buy lunch since.

Stephen Venables, on how climbing Everest had changed his life

He who dies with the most toes, wins.

Greg Mushial, climber, on frostbite

COLLEGE FOOTBALL

College football is a game which would be much more interesting if the faculty played instead of the students, and even more interesting if the trustees played. There would be a great increase in broken arms, legs, and necks, and simultaneously an appreciable diminution in the loss to humanity.

H. L. Mencken, wit

College football is a sport that bears the same relation to education that bullfighting does to agriculture.

Elbert Hubbard, wit

At my institution we're determined to develop a school of which the football team can be proud.

Anon.

It's reassuring that colleges are putting the emphasis on education again. One school has gotten so strict that they won't give a football player his letter unless he can tell them which one it is.

Henny Youngman, comedian

Twenty books have been destroyed in a fire at Auburn University's football dorm. But the real tragedy was that fifteen of them hadn't been colored in yet.

> Steve Spurrier, head coach of the University of South
> Carolina Gamecocks

See also: AMERICAN FOOTBALL, CHEERLEADERS

COMMENTATORS AND BROADCASTERS

In his quieter moments, he sounds as if his trousers are on fire.

Clive James, on motor racing commentator Murray Walker

If you're a sporting star, you're a sporting star. If you don't quite make it, you become a coach. If you can't coach, you become a journalist. If you can't spell, you introduce *Grandstand* on a Saturday afternoon.

Des Lynam, BBC *Grandstand* presenter

Des Lynam is so laid back, he's almost horizontal. Which is exactly how his legion of fantasising housewifely fans imagine him to be.

Frank Keating, sports journalist, on BBC presenter

McCarver is the pre-eminent over-analyst of his day. Ask him what time it is and he'll tell you how a watch works. He can do twenty minutes on the height of the infield grass.

Norman Chad, of TV sports presenter Tim McCarver, *Sports Illustrated*, 1992

John McCririck ... looking like a hedge dragged through a man backwards.

Sunday Express, on Channel 4 commentator

John is one man who doesn't let success go to his clothes.
  Mike Ditka, NFL player, commentator and coach, on
  football commentator John Madden

Prats – talking, writing and pontificating about things of which they know nothing – are the curse of modern sport. And I definitely include prominent former sportsmen, in fact they are the worst of all.
  Andy Ripley, England rugby union player and
  all-round athlete

Hubie was to network ratings what the *Titanic* was to the winter cruise business.
  Pat Williams, Orlando Magic general manager, on basketball commentator Hubie Brown

A color commentator is a guy who is paid to talk while everyone goes to the bathroom.
  Bill Curry, American football coach

GAFFES AND BLOOPERS

You can hear the hush of expectancy buzzing around the ground.
  Colin Murray, BBC commentator

Remember, postcards only, please. The winner will be the first one opened.
  Brian Moore, broadcaster

Well, that kind of puts the damper on even a Yankees win.
   Phil Rizzuto, New York Yankees shortstop and announcer,
   after announcing the death of Pope Paul VI

Commentating isn't as simple as it sounds.
   Ted Lowe, BBC commentator

See also: NEWSPAPERS

CRICKET

Cricket Explained – 1

You have two sides, one out in the field and one in. Each man in the side that's in, goes out and when he's out, he comes in and the next man goes in until he's out.

When they're all out, the side that's out comes in and the side that's been in goes out and tries to get those coming in out.

Sometimes you get men still in and not out. When both sides have been in and out, including not outs, that's the end of the game.

Cricket Explained – 2

Two old men in white coats walk together to the middle of a large green field, each carrying three long sticks and two little ones.

Each plants his three sticks in the ground, 22 yards apart and puts the little sticks on top.

They then turn around and look towards twenty-two younger men at the edge of the field – and it starts to rain.

Anon.

Cricket: casting the ball at three straight sticks and defending the same with a fourth.

Rudyard Kipling, writer and poet

I watched a cricket match for three hours waiting for it to start.

    Groucho Marx, actor and comedian

The last positive thing England did for cricket was to invent it.

    Ian Chappell, Australian captain

Cricket is the only game that you can actually put on weight when playing.

    Tommy Docherty, Scottish footballer and manager

I have never got over the shock of seeing my first cricket ball. I simply couldn't believe that there was anything so dangerous loose in what up to then had seemed a safe sort of world.

    Robert Morley, actor and wit

Don't blame the bloody pitch, it's not the pitch. It's the fact they can't play on it, that's the problem.

    Colin Graves, Yorkshire chairman after their relegation to Division Two

We know you can lose wickets in clusters and we seem to have lost ten there in a cluster.

    Alastair Cook, England batsman and captain, following an England defeat by India

It is like giving a machine gun to a monkey. It can be fantastic or it can be an absolute disaster too.

    Hugh Morris, cricketer and administrator, on the problems with players tweeting

If Botham is an English folk hero, then this must be an alarming time for the nation.

David Miller of Ian Botham

Freddie Flintoff's sparkling earring looks utterly ridiculous. Like an Old-Etonian tie on an orang-utan.

Peter McKay, columnist

A loving wife is better than making 50 at cricket or even 99; beyond that I will not go.

J. M. Barrie, author and dramatist

Any sport which goes on for so long that you might need a 'comfort break' is not a sport at all. It is merely a means of passing the time. Like reading.

Jeremy Clarkson, motoring journalist

I bowl so slow that if after I have delivered the ball and don't like the look of it, I can run after it and bring it back.

J. M. Barrie

Personally, I have always looked upon cricket as organised loafing.

William Temple, Archbishop of Canterbury, 1925

When you can watch Inter Milan vs. Barcelona, why on earth would you want to watch Chennai Chunderers vs. Delhi Dipsticks?

David Lloyd, Lancashire and England cricketer and commentator, on the Indian Premier League

There is nothing in cricket more calculated to raise a laugh than the sight of some determined and serious man under a spiralling catch.

Peter Roebuck, *Tangled up in White*, 1990

For six days, thou shall push up and down the line, but on the seventh day thou shall swipe.

Doug Padgett, Yorkshire and England batsman

When you win the toss – bat. If you are in doubt, think about it, then bat. If you have very big doubts, consult a colleague – then bat.

W. G. Grace, attrib.

After years of patient study (and with cricket there can be no other kind), I have decided that there is nothing wrong with the game that the introduction of golf carts wouldn't fix in a hurry.

Bill Bryson, *Down Under*, 2000

Cricket needs brightening up a bit. My solution is to let players drink at the beginning of the game, not after. It always works in our picnic matches.

Paul Hogan, comedian

It is not true that the English invented cricket as a way of making all other human endeavours look interesting and lively; that was merely an unintended side effect. I don't wish to denigrate a sport that is enjoyed by millions, some of them awake and facing the right way, but it is an odd game.

Bill Bryson, *Down Under*, 2000

Cricket is just baseball on Valium.

Robin Williams, American actor and comedian

And when you rub the ball on rump or belly,
Remember what it looks like on the telly.

A. P. Herbert, wit

Devon Malcolm is the scattergun of Test cricket, capable on his worst days of putting the fear of God into short leg and second slip rather than the batsman. But sometimes, when the force is with him and he puts his contact lenses in the correct eyes, he can be devastating.

Mike Selvey, *The Guardian*

I see that Northamptonshire have a new bowler called Kettle. May I suggest to Keith Andrew that the best time to put him on would be ten minutes before the tea interval.

Letter to *The Cricketer*

Only his mother would describe him as an athlete.

Derek Pringle of Ashley Giles, England cricketer

A fast bowler so hot-headed it was a surprise his sun hat never burst into flames.

Harry Pearson of John Snow, England bowler

He's bowled like a camel and fielded like a drain.

Bob Willis of Kabir Ali, English pace bowler

Sixteen needed from two overs. If we win, jubilation; if we lose, despair. It matters not how we played the game, but whether we won – or lost.

Vic Marks, player, cricket writer and BBC commentator, on limited-over cricket

Jason Gillespie is a 30-year-old in a 36-year-old body.
  Bob Willis, England bowler

They said to me at the Oval, come and see our new bowling machine. 'Bowling machine?' I said, 'I used to be the bowling machine.'
  Alec Bedser, Surrey and England bowler

When I get to heaven I shall produce on my behalf, in hope of salvation, my stock of failures and frustrations. My attempt to become a leader writer on the *Manchester Guardian*, my attempts to sing the 'Abschied' of Wotan, my attempts to understand Hegel, my attempts to spin a fast ball from the leg to the off stump.
  Neville Cardus, cricket writer

Watching cricket is easy. All anyone needs is a deckchair, a pipe or knitting, and a week off from the office.
  Time magazine

My wife had an uncle who could never walk down the nave of his abbey without wondering whether it would take spin.
  Lord Home, *The Twentieth Century Revisited*, BBC TV, 1982

Cricket is a game which the British, not being a spiritual people, had to invent in order to have some concept of eternity.
  Lord Mancroft, English politician

I used to play under the worst captain ever. He always used to put me in to bat in the middle of a hat trick!
  Anon.

I cannot for the life of me see why the umpires, the only two people on a cricket field who are not going to get grass stains on their knees, are the only two people allowed to wear dark trousers.

Katharine Whitehorn, journalist

If there were an Olympic event for running backwards, I would be the obvious favourite.

Harold 'Dickie' Bird, cricket umpire

Sir Donald Bradman,
Would have been a very glad man,
If his Test average had been .06 more,
Than 99.94.

T. N. E. Smith, poet

To those who insist on asking who was the greatest batsman, Trumper or Bradman, I feel the only fitting answer is another question: which was the finer seaman, Sinbad the Sailor or Popeye the Sailorman?

Raymond Robinson, *From the Boundary*, 1951

Many continentals think life is a game, the English think cricket is a game.

George Mikes, *How to be an Alien*, 1946

It's a funny kind of month, October. For the really keen cricket fan it's when you discover that your wife left you in May.

Denis Norden, writer, *She*, 1977

Taking a cricket ball away from Clarrie Grimmett during a match was like taking a bone from a dog.

R. S. Whittington, cricket writer, of Australian spin bowler

Everyone knows which comes first when it's a question of cricket or sex – all discerning people recognise that.

Harold Pinter, playwright

You can have sex either before cricket or after cricket – the fundamental fact is that cricket must be there at the centre of things.

Harold Pinter, *Pinter on Pinter*, 1980

Oh God, if there be cricket in heaven, let there also be rain.

Sir Alec Douglas-Home, British Prime Minister, attrib.

I do not play cricket because it requires me to assume such indecent positions.

Oscar Wilde, playwright

I smiled at Ricky Ponting. He didn't smile back. He was in a terrible temper for some reason. Quite why he was blaming me when his partner, Damien Martyn, had called him for a suicidal single to cover, I don't know. You know what's more? All the palaver caused me to burn my toast.

Duncan Fletcher, Zimbabwean player and England coach, on the fallout from the infamous Gary Pratt run-out

They bring him out of the loft, take the dust sheet off, give him a pink gin and sit him there. He can't go out of a 30-mile radius of London because he's usually too pissed to get back. He sits there at Lord's saying: 'That's Botham, look at his hair, they tell me he's had some of that cannabis stuff.'

Ian Botham, cricketer, on the stereotypical England selector

He's decided to give up first-class cricket. But he'll still be playing for Australia.
Anon.

Like an elephant trying to do the pole vault.
Jonathan Agnew, commentator, as heavyweight Pakistan captain Inzamam-ul-Haq falls over his own stumps

Botham just couldn't quite get his leg over.
Jonathan Agnew, as Ian Botham tries vainly to lift his leg over his stumps when off balance

I've never got to the bottom of streaking.
Jonathan Agnew

Ray Jennings was to orthodoxy what King Herod was to child-minding.
Mike Atherton, cricketer, writer and commentator, on the South African coach

The only one who really got up my nose was Steve Waugh, who spent the entire series giving out verbals. A bit of a joke really when he was the one bloke wetting himself against the quick bowlers.
Mike Atherton, on Australian batsman and captain

The number of fumbles, misfields and grabs at thin air brought to mind some England performances of the past ... a team full of dobbers and crap fielders? It has been said about every England touring team to Australia in the past fifteen years. It's nice to be able to return the compliment.
Mike Atherton

It looks more suitable for growing carrots.
>   Andy Atkinson, ICC grounds inspector, on Bermuda's
>   new pitch

Tufnell! Can I borrow your brain? I'm building an idiot.
>   Australian fan to England spinner Phil Tufnell

Leaving out Dennis Lillee against England would be as
unthinkable as the Huns dropping Attila.
>   Australian TV commentator

Well, Andrew Strauss is certainly an optimist – he's come
out wearing sunblock.
>   Australian commentator in the Fifth Test of the 5–0 series
>   whitewash in 2006–7

England trained and grass grew at the MCG yesterday,
two activities virtually indistinguishable from each other
in tempo.
>   Greg Baum, Australian sports journalist

It was an excellent performance in the field marred only
when Harris dropped Crapp in the outfield.
>   BBC commentator, on a missed chance off batsman
>   Jack Crapp

How can you tell your wife you are just popping out to play
a match and then not come back for five days?
>   Rafa Benitez, Spanish football manager, struggling to come
>   to terms with Test cricket

England's pace bowlers are making the helmet go out
of fashion.
>   Scyld Berry, English cricket writer

Richie Benaud simply says 'out' with the grisly finality of the hangman.

Tony Brace

Merv Hughes always appeared to be wearing a tumble-dried ferret on his top lip.

Rick Broadbent, sportswriter

Too high?! If the ball had hit his head it would have hit the bloody wickets!

Alan Brown, Kent cricketer, denied an LBW appeal against
Lancashire's 5ft 3in Harry Pilling

We had one or two disagreements but once he realised that he was wrong and I was right we moved on.

Alan Butcher, Surrey coach, on working with his son Mark

I once delivered a simple ball, which I was told, had it gone far enough, would have been considered a wide.

Lewis Carroll, writer

I can't really say I'm batting badly. I'm not batting long enough to be batting badly.

Greg Chappell, Australian Test captain

The other advantage England have got when Phil Tufnell is bowling is that he isn't fielding.

Ian Chappell

In my day fifty-eight beers between London and Sydney would have virtually classified you as a teetotaller.

Ian Chappell, after batsman David Boon drank fifty-eight
cans of beer on the flight from Australia to England

Three bad days does not mean you're a bad team overnight.
  Paul Collingwood, English Test cricketer

Now Botham, with a chance to put everything that's gone before behind him.
  Tony Cozier, commentator

Angus Fraser's bowling is like shooting down F-16 aeroplanes with sling shots. Even if they hit, no damage would be done. Like an old horse, he should be put out to pasture.
  Colin Croft, West Indies bowler and broadcaster

I can't bat, can't bowl and can't field these days. I've every chance of being picked for England.
  Ray East, Essex cricketer

It's difficult being more laid back than David Gower without actually being comatose.
  Frances Edmonds, cricket writer

Ian Botham is in no way inhibited by a capacity to over-intellectualise.
  Frances Edmonds

He's got a reputation for being awkward and arrogant, probably because he is awkward and arrogant.
  Frances Edmonds, on her husband Phil, England cricketer

I want to play cricket, it doesn't seem to matter if you win or lose.
  Meat Loaf, singer

It would be extremely difficult for me to choose between singing Elvis Presley songs and scoring a century for England, but I think I would choose a century for England.

Tim Rice, composer and amateur cricketer

He played his cricket on the heath.
The pitch was full of bumps.
A fast ball hit him on the teeth,
The dentist drew the stumps.

Anon.

A dry fart!

Phil Edmonds, England bowler, on being asked what he looked forward to most upon returning from a long tour of India

You know Lords? Well, once I played there,
And a ball I hit to leg –
Struck the umpire's head and stayed there,
As a nest retains an egg.
Hastily the wicket-keeper
Seized a stump and prized about;
Had it gone two inches deeper
He would ne'er have run me out.
This I minded all the more
As my stroke was well worth four.

Harry Graham, *Ruthless Rhymes*, 1899

Cricket is a tough and terrible rough unscrupulous game. No wonder our American friends do not like it.

A. P. Herbert, speech at Surrey County Cricket Club dinner

John Jameson is expressionless and big. Big in the way they used to describe barrel chested; which means that he looks as if he is permanently holding his breath.

Clive Taylor, sports journalist, of England wicketkeeper

English crowds are like sherry. West Indian crowds are like rum. Australian crowds are like Foster's.

Peter Roebuck, *Tangled up in White*, 1990

They should have been a last line of defence during the war. It would have been made up entirely of the most officious breed of cricket stewards. If Hitler had tried to invade these shores he would have been met by a short, stout man in a white coat who would have said, 'I don't care who you are, you're not coming in here unless you are a member!'

Ray East

Derek Randall bats like an octopus with piles.

Matthew Engel, cricket writer

Waugh! What is he good for? Absolutely nothing!

England fans' song during the 1993 Ashes series

It means I can drive a flock of sheep through the town centre, drink for free in no less than sixty-four pubs and get a lift home with the police when I become inebriated. What more could you want?

Andrew Flintoff, England cricketer, on being awarded the freedom of Preston

I'm completely different from Pietersen. He would turn up to the opening of an envelope.

Andrew Flintoff, on his teammate Kevin Pietersen

It's far more daunting than bowling to Ricky Ponting or facing Shane Warne.

> Andrew Flintoff, on news that he was to duet with Elton John

In the past five weeks I've trained hard, trying to get my ankle back to where I want it to be.

> Andrew Flintoff

I'm ugly, I'm overweight, but I'm happy.

> Andrew Flintoff

Lady, if I were built in proportion I'd be 8 foot 10!

> Joel Garner, West Indies bowler

Srikkanth is a vegetarian. If he swallows a fly, he will be in trouble.

> Sunil Gavaskar, Indian opening batsman on his teammate

This is Cunis at the Vauxhall End. Cunis – a funny sort of name. Neither one thing nor the other.

> Alan Gibson, commentator

A fart competing with thunder.

> Graham Gooch, former England batsman, assessing
> England vs. Australia ahead of the 1990/91 Ashes

If it had been a cheese roll, it would have never got past him.

> Graham Gooch, after Mike Gatting was bowled by Shane
> Warne's 'Ball of the Century'

Illy [former England captain Ray Illingworth] had the man-management skills of Basil Fawlty.

> Darren Gough, England bowler

I don't know an England player who could fix a light bulb, let alone a match.

Darren Gough

Border is a walnut: hard to crack and without much to please the eye.

Peter Roebuck, cricketer and writer, on Australian captain
Allan Border

When Justin Langer finds his off stump akimbo he leaves the crease only after asking the Met Office whether any earthquakes have been recorded in the region. In any case, he never edges the ball. It's just that his bat handle keeps breaking.

Peter Roebuck

An ordinary bloke trying to make good without ever losing the air of a fellow with a hangover.

Peter Roebuck, on Australia's Merv Hughes

It's hard work making batting look effortless.

David Gower, England batsman

I don't like defensive shots – you can only get threes.

W. G. Grace, Victorian England batsman

They came to see me bat not you bowl.

W. G. Grace, putting the bails back on his stumps after
being bowled first ball

Being the manager of a touring team is rather like being in charge of a cemetery – lots of people underneath you, but no one listening.

Wes Hall, West Indian bowler and administrator

Ashley Giles made a simple attempt at a top-edged hook by Mahela Jayawardene look like a *Mr Bean* Christmas special.
  Peter Hayter, commentator, lamenting the standard of England's fielding, 2003

Shane Warne's idea of a balanced diet is a cheeseburger in each hand.
  Ian Heath, cricket writer

Mate, if you just turn the bat over, you'll find instructions on the other side.
  Merv Hughes, Australian fast bowler, to Robin Smith after the England batsman repeatedly played and missed

The sight of Imran [Khan] tearing fearsomely down the hill and the baying of the crowd made me realise for the first time that adrenalin was sometimes brown.
  Simon Hughes, English cricketer, writer and commentator

Dermot Reeve was so self-obsessed that even on the local nudist beach he only admired himself.
  Simon Hughes, on his teammate

You don't need a helmet facing Waqar [Younis] so much as a steel toe cap.
  Simon Hughes, on Pakistani fast bowler Waqar Younis's inswinging yorker

Clinching the [County] Championship is a strange sensation... There's more atmosphere in a doctor's waiting room.
  Simon Hughes

As harrowing occupations go, there can't be much to choose between the Australian cricket captaincy and social work on Skid Row.

    Doug Ibbotson, *Daily Telegraph* cricket writer

I have on occasion taken a quite reasonable dislike to the Australians.

    Ted Dexter, England captain and commentator

Shane Warne is thicker than a complete set of *Wisden* yearbooks.

    Matt Price, Australian newspaper columnist

The sound of the ball hitting the batsman's skull was music to my ears.

    Jeff Thomson, Australian fast bowler

I absolutely insist that all my boys are in bed before breakfast.

    Colin Ingleby-Mackenzie explaining how Hampshire won
    the County Championship under his captaincy

I haven't noticed too many comments about my Aussie background out in the middle, but that's probably because I haven't been batting long enough to notice!

    Geraint Jones, Australian raised England cricketer

Don't bowl him bad balls, he hits the good ones for fours.

    Michael Kasprowicz, Australian bowler on Indian batsman
    Sachin Tendulkar

A 1914 biplane tied up with elastic bands trying vainly to take off.

>Frank Keating, sports journalist, on Bob Willis's
>bowling action

The programme implied that ... he made love like he played cricket: slowly, methodically, but with the real possibility that he might stay in all day.

>Martin Kelner, legendary *Guardian* columnist and
>radio presenter, reviewing a TV documentary about
>Geoffrey Boycott

An interesting morning, full of interest.

>Jim Laker, England bowler and commentator

And Ian Greig's on eight, including two fours.

>Jim Laker

It's a unique occasion really – a repeat of Melbourne 1977.

>Jim Laker

Sometimes people think it's like polo, played on horseback, and I remember one guy thought it was a game involving insects.

>Clayton Lambert, West Indies and American batsman, on
>explaining cricket to Americans

England have no McGrathish bowlers, there are hardly any McGrathish bowlers – except for [Glenn] McGrath.

>Stuart Law, Australian cricketer and coach

There's nothing like the sound of flesh on leather to get a cricket match going.
  Geoff Lawson, Australian cricketer and coach

For any budding cricketers listening, do you have any superstitious routines before an innings, like putting one pad on first and then the other one?
  Tony Lewis, Welsh cricketer and broadcaster

If I've to bowl to Sachin [Tendulkar], I'll bowl with a helmet on. He hits the ball so hard.
  Dennis Lillee, Australian fast bowler

Geoffrey [Boycott] is the only fellow I've ever met who fell in love with himself at a young age and has remained faithful ever since.
  Dennis Lillee

They've got to swing like a '70s disco to get anywhere near from here.
  David Lloyd, on an Essex Twenty20 run chase

If this bloke's a Test match bowler, then my backside is a fire engine.
  David Lloyd, on first seeing New Zealander Nathan Astle

What do I think of the reverse sweep? It's like Manchester United getting a penalty and Bryan Robson taking it with his head.
  David Lloyd

England have nothing to lose here, apart from this Test match.
  David Lloyd

She was a lovely lady and quite ample. In fact, Muttiah Muralitharan would have had plenty of room to sign his name.
  David Lloyd, asked to sign a woman's cleavage

Ian Botham: Where were you last night?
David Lloyd: An oyster bar – apparently it puts lead in your pencil. I don't know about that. I think it only matters if you have got someone to write to.

It was rather a pity Ellis got run out at 1107, because I was just striking a length.
  Arthur Mailey, New South Wales bowler who took 4-362
  during Victoria's first-class record score in 1926/7

... two by a man in the pavilion wearing a bowler hat and one by an unfortunate teammate whom he consoled with the words, 'I'm expecting to take a wicket any day now.'
  Arthur Mailey, who said that his figures would have been
  much better 'had not three sitters been dropped off his
  bowling'

The enigma with no variation.
  Vic Marks, on Chris Lewis, England all-rounder

I suppose I can gain some consolation from the fact that my name will be permanently in the record books.
  Malcolm Nash, Glamorgan bowler, after being hit for six
  sixes in an over by Gary Sobers in 1968

His claim of being an all-rounder is clearly more a reflection of his physique than abilities in Test cricket.
  Bangladesh newspaper on captain Khaled Mahmud

If my grandfather was alive, he would have slaughtered a cow.

> Makhaya Ntini, South African bowler, after taking 5-75
> against England at Lord's

Boy George would be considered straight at the University of Western Australia.

> Kerry O'Keefe casting doubts about the tests done by the
> University on Sri Lankan Muttiah Muralitharan's contro-
> versial bowling action

Andre Nel is big and raw-boned and I suspect he has the IQ of an empty swimming pool.

> Adam Parore, New Zealand wicketkeeper, on South
> African fast bowler

Sorry, skipper, a leopard can't change its stripes.

> Lennie Pascoe, Australian fast bowler

It's a Catch-21 situation.

> Kevin Pietersen, England batsman

No good hitting me there, mate, there's nothing to damage.

> Derek Randall, England cricketer, to Australia's Dennis
> Lillee after being hit on the head by a bouncer

The blackcurrant jam tastes of fish to me.

> Derek Randall, tasting caviar for the first time

There's only one man made more appeals than you, George, and that was Dr Barnardo.

> Bill Reeve, umpire, to George Macaulay, England bowler

Umpire Eddie Nichols is a man who cannot find his own buttocks with his two hands.

Navjot Sidhu, Indian batsman and commentator

The third umpires should be changed as often as nappies ... and for the same reason.

Navjot Sidhu

He played that like a dwarf at a urinal.

Navjot Sidhu, as Sachin Tendulkar stands on his tocs to play a shot

Yorkshire were 232 all out, Hutton ill. No, I'm sorry, Hutton 111.

John Snagge, BBC broadcaster

We've won one on the trot.

Alec Stewart, England cricketer

You can't smoke twenty a day and bowl fast.

Phil Tufnell, Middlesex and England bowler, on why he became a spinner

My main aim as far as practice went was to turn up on time in order to avoid another fine from the management.

Phil Tufnell

I've done the elephant, I've done the poverty. I might as well go home.

Phil Tufnell, on a tour in India

My knee is fine, but my neck hurts from watching all the sixes hit by Australia.
  Michael Vaughan, Yorkshire and England batsman, at the
  2007 Twenty20 series

Richie Benaud eyes the camera with the look of a disdainful lizard.
  Brian Viner, British sportswriter

He has got perfect control over the ball right up to the minute he lets it go.
  Peter Walker, Glamorgan and England bowler, batsman
  and commentator

With the possible exception of Rolf Harris, no other Australian has inflicted more pain and grief on Englishmen since Don Bradman.
  Mike Walters, British sports reporter, at Steve Waugh's
  retirement

We slept under the stars in sleeping bags – it was wonderful getting bitten by the mozzies – I'm still covered in bites. We went orienteering in the middle of the night with 6-foot kangaroos jumping around. It was just a wonderful time!
  Shane Warne, Australian bowler, on coach John Buchanan's
  'boot camp'

I'm a big believer that the coach is something you travel in to get to and from the game.
  Shane Warne, speaking about coach John Buchanan

The traditional dress of the Australian cricketer is the baggy green cap on the head and the chip on the shoulder. Both are ritualistically assumed.

Simon Barnes, *The Times*

So dull is he, that tapes of the Willis delivery should be sold in Mothercare as a sleeping aid for fractious toddlers.

Jim White, sportswriter, on Bob Willis's style of commentary

Kevin Pietersen would be deemed brash by a Texan assertiveness coach.

Simon Wilde, English cricket writer

The aim of English cricket is, in fact, mainly to beat Australia.

Jim Laker

His wife was in full flow: 'Cricket, cricket, cricket – that's all you think about. What about us? I bet you couldn't even tell me what day we were married!'

'Yes I could,' replied the husband. 'It was the day Botham scored 145 against the Australians!'

Anon.

The only time an Australian ever walks is when his car runs out of petrol.

Barry Richards, South African batsman

There would have been serious trouble between David and Jonathan if either had persisted in dropping catches off the other's bowling.

P. G. Wodehouse

If you're playing against the Australians you don't walk.
  Ian Botham

Our wicketkeeper is absolutely hopeless. The only thing he caught all season was whooping cough.
  Anon.

A leg cutter is a delivery which batsmen play and miss at outside off-stump when Richie Benaud is commentating.
  Vic Marks

How do you mean, you had to explain the cricket match to your wife?
She found out I wasn't there.
  Anon.

Why do they call it a hat-trick?
Because it's always performed by a bowler.
  Anon.

I guess some guys are just naturally built for comfort rather than cricket.
  Bob Willis, on Robert Key, Kent and England batsman

Most teams you know only the next player to bat puts the pads on. With Zimbabwe, everyone puts pads on!
  Zimbabwe supporter

I was once offered a Foster's from someone over the fence – but it was warmer and frothier than a Foster's.
  Bob Willis

Go on Hedley, you've got him in two minds, he doesn't know whether to hit you for four or six.

Arthur Wood, to England teammate Hedley Verity

Sledging

Greg Thomas: It's red, round and weighs about five ounces if you're wondering.

After Greg Thomas beat Viv Richards on the outside edge a couple of times

Viv Richards: Greg, you know what it looks like. Now go and find it.

Richards hit the very next ball for six, out of the ground and into a river

Hell, Gatt, move out the way! I can't see the wickets.

Dennis Lillee, after stopping in mid run-up to bowl to Mike Gatting

Are you going to get out or do I have to come round the wicket and kill you?

Malcolm Marshall, West Indies fast bowler to David Boon, Australian batsman

What do you think this is, a f**king tea party? No you can't have a f**king glass of water. You can f**king wait like all the rest of us.

Allan Border, to Robin Smith

So how's your wife and my kids?

Rodney Marsh to Ian Botham in an Ashes match

The wife's fine. The kids are retarded!
>   Ian Botham's reply

You've got to bat on this in a minute, Tufnell. Hospital food
suit you?
>   Craig McDermott, Australian bowler, to Phil Tufnell

Which one of you bastards called this bastard a bastard?
>   England captain Douglas Jardine complained that one of
>   the Australian players called him a bastard. Australian
>   captain Bill Woodfull turned to his team, pointed to Jardine
>   and asked the above questions.

Shane Warne: I've waited two years for another chance to
humiliate you.
Daryll Cullinan: Looks like you spent it eating.
>   Australian bowler to South African batsman

I have prepared for the worst case scenario, but it could be
even worse than that.
>   Monty Panesar, England spinner, ready to face abuse
>   in Australia

Aussie sledging? I'm just glad they've heard of me!
>   Monty Panesar

Mark Waugh: F**k me, look who it is. Mate, what are you
doing out here, there's no way you're good enough to play
for England.
Jimmy Ormond: Maybe not, but at least I'm the best player
in my family.

Merv is a funny guy, though he would sledge his own mother if he thought it would help the cause.

Gladstone Small, England bowler on Australian bowler
Merv Hughes

John Arlott – Cricket Writer and Broadcaster

Like an old lady poking with her umbrella at a wasp's nest.

On the batting of Australian Ernie Toshack

Alan Butcher drops his head, both hands behind his back and looks sheepishly down the wicket like a small boy caught stealing jam.

Lillee is wearing a voluminous nightshirt which would have room for another man, if he could get into the trousers.

A stroke of a man knocking a thistle top with a walking stick.

On a Clive Lloyd four

What we have here is a clear case of Mann's inhumanity to Mann.

Commenting on South African bowler 'Tufty' Mann causing England batsman George Mann problems

The umpire signals a bye with the air of a weary stork.

Bill Frindall has done a bit of mental arithmetic with a calculator.

He played a cut so late as to be positively posthumous.

The fieldsmen are scattered in the wilderness like missionaries.

It is rather suitable for umpires to dress like dentists, since one of their tasks is to draw stumps.

Ian Botham – England Test Player and Commentator

A few years ago England would have struggled to beat the Eskimos.

I don't ask my wife to face Michael Holding, so there's no reason why I should be changing nappies.

I don't think I've actually drunk a beer for fifteen years, except a few Guinnesses in Dublin, where it's the law.

This can only help England's cause.
    On hearing that Geoffrey Boycott was to coach the
    Pakistan batsmen before their 2001 tour of England

I'd rather face Dennis Lillee with a stick of rhubarb than go through that again.
    After being cleared of assault charges

If I'd done a quarter of the things of which I'm accused, I'd be pickled in alcohol, I'd be a registered drug addict and would have sired half the children in the world's cricket-playing countries.

It couldn't have been Gatt. Anything he takes up to his room after nine o'clock, he eats.
    On the Mike Gatting barmaid scandal

I've had about ten operations. I'm a bit like a battered old Escort. You might find one panel left that's original.

Cricket is full of theorists who can ruin your game in no time.

Pakistan is the sort of place every man should send his mother-in-law to, for a month, all expenses paid.

Botham? I could have bowled him out with a cabbage, with the outside leaves still on.

> Cec Pepper, Australian all-rounder

Geoffrey Boycott – England Test Player and Commentator

I reckon my mum could have caught that in her pinny!

> On a dropped catch

He could have caught that between the cheeks of his backside.

> On a second dropped catch

I feel so bad about mine now I'm going to tie it around the cat.

> Dismayed at the award of an MBE to Paul Collingwood
> for scoring 17 runs in the 2005 Ashes series

Norman Cowans should remember what happened to Graham Dilley, who started off as a genuinely quick bowler. Then, they started stuffing line and length into his ear, and now he has Dennis Lillee's action with Denis Thatcher's pace.

To have some idea what it's like, stand in the outside lane of a motorway, get your mate to drive his car at you at 95mph and wait until he's twelve yards away before you decide which way to jump.

On facing fast bowlers

My tactic would be to take a quick single and observe him from the other end.

On how to play Shane Warne or Glenn McGrath

They should cut Joel Garner off at the knees to make him bowl at a normal height.

Of the West Indies fast bowler

Geoff Boycott's idea of bliss might be to bat all night, having batted all day.

John Woodcock, cricket writer

Martin Johnson – Cricket Writer

Ilott is out of this game with a groin strain and thus joins Darren Gough, Chris Lewis and Andrew Caddick on the list of those more in line for a trip to Lourdes rather than Lord's.

At least we are safe from an intoxicating rendition of 'There's only one Graeme Hick'. There are, quite clearly, two of them. The first one turns out for teams like Worcestershire and New Zealand's Northern Districts and plays like a god. The second one pulls on an England cap and plays like an anagram of god.

Michael Atherton is one of the few people capable of looking more dishevelled at the start of a six-hour century than at the end of it.

The mincing run-up resembles someone in high heels and a panty girdle chasing after a bus.
   On Australian bowler Merv Hughes

It would be a surprise if the mirrors in [Kevin] Pietersen's house totalled anything less than the entire stock at one of the larger branches of B&Q.

As a preparation for a Test match, the domestic game is the equivalent of training for the Olympic marathon by taking the dog for a walk.

How anyone can spin a ball the width of [Mike] Gatting boggles the mind.
   On Shane Warne's 'Ball of the Century'

If he's not talking about the flipper it's the zooter, the slider, or the wrong'un. He'll shortly start working on a ball that loops the loop, disappears down his trouser leg, and whistles 'Waltzing Matilda' before rattling into the stumps.
   On Shane Warne

Fraser's approach to the wicket currently resembles someone who has his braces caught in the sightscreen.
   Of Angus Fraser, England bowler

Brian Johnston – BBC Commentator

Batsmen wear so much protection these days that I mostly identify them from their posteriors.
Bill [Frindall] needs a small ruler. How about the Sultan of Brunei? I hear he is only 4 foot 10.

Fred Trueman – England Test Cricketer and Commentator

There's only one head bigger than Tony Greig's – and that's Birkenhead.

I know why Boycott's bought a house by the sea – so he'll be able to go for a walk on the water.

Kid yourself it's Sunday, Rev, and keep your hands together.
    After Rev. David Sheppard dropped a succession
    of catches

I'm all right when his arm comes over, but I'm out of form by the time the bloody ball gets here.
    On the slow bowling of Peter Sainsbury

England's always expecting. No wonder they call her the Mother Country.

Subba Row: I'm sorry about that, it might have been better if I had kept my legs together.
Trueman: Aye, it's a pity your mother didn't!
    After the ball which Raman Subba Row had dropped off
    Trueman's bowling had gone for four

You might keep your eyes shut when your praying, Vicar, but I wish you'd keep 'em open when I'm bowling.

    After the Rev. David Sheppard had dropped a catch off his bowling

I'd throw them off the top of the pavilion. Mind you, I'm a fair man, I'd give them a 50–50 chance. I'd have Keith Fletcher underneath trying to catch them.

    On the saboteurs who dug up the Headingley Test wicket

The Definitive Volume on the Finest Bloody Fast Bowler that Ever Drew Breath.

    Suggested title for his autobiography

GAFFES AND BLOOPERS

After their 60 overs, West Indies have scored 244 for 7, all out.

    Frank Bough, sports broadcaster

I'm glad two sides of the cherry have been put forward.

    Geoffrey Boycott, English player and commentator

That's a remarkable catch by Yardley especially as the ball quite literally rolled along the ground towards him.

    Mike Denness, Scottish batsman and commentator

The Queen's Park Oval, exactly as its name suggests – absolutely round.

    Tony Cozier

The ball came back, literally cutting Graham Thorpe in half.

    Colin Croft

Who could forget Malcolm Devon?

> Ted Dexter, completely forgetting Devon Malcolm's name

Interviewer: Do you feel that the selectors and yourself have been vindicated by the result?
Mike Gatting: I don't think the press are vindictive. They can write what they want.

Glenn McGrath joins Craig McDermott and Paul Reiffel in a three-ponged prace attack.

> Tim Gavel, Australian sports broadcaster

In the back of Hughes's mind must be the thought that he will dance down the piss and mitch one.

> Tony Greig, batsman and commentator

Clearly the West Indies are going to play their normal game, which is what they normally do.

> Tony Greig

What a magnificent shot! No, he's out.

> Tony Greig

A very small crowd here today. I can count the people on one hand. Can't be more than thirty.

> Michael Abrahamson, commentator

[Geoffrey] Boycott, somewhat a creature of habit, likes exactly the sort of food he himself prefers.

> Don Mosey, BBC commentator

If you go in with two fast bowlers and one breaks down, you're left two short.

> Bob Massie, Australian bowler

I'm confident they play the game in heaven. Wouldn't be heaven otherwise would it?

Patrick Moore, astronomer

I've seen batting all over the world. And in other countries too.

Keith Miller, Australian all-rounder

Michael Vaughan has a long history in the game ahead of him.

Mark Nicholas, British commentator

This game will be over anytime from now.

Alan McGilvray, Australian commentator

Well, everyone is enjoying this except Vic Marks, and I think he's enjoying himself.

Don Mosey

It's a perfect day here in Australia, glorious blue sunshine.

Christopher Martin-Jenkins, BBC commentator

And we don't need a calculator to tell us that the required run-rate is 4.5454 per over.

Christopher Martin-Jenkins

Gul has another ball in his hand and bowls to Bell who has two.

Christopher Martin-Jenkins, on Pakistan's Umar Gul

We have had exceptionally wet weather in Derby – everywhere in the county is in the same boat.

Tom Sears, administrator for Cricket Kenya

This ground is surprising. It holds about 60,000 but when there are around 30,000 in, you get the feeling that it is half empty.

Ravi Shastri, Indian all-rounder

A brain scan revealed that Andrew Caddick is not suffering from a fracture of the shin.

Jo Sheldon, British broadcaster

The only change England would propose might be to replace Derek Pringle, who remains troubled by no balls.

The Times

With regard to the broken finger, when batting I'll just have to play it by ear.

Marcus Trescothick, Somerset and England batsman

I just want to get into the middle and get the right sort of runs.

Robin Smith, suffering from diarrhoea on an England tour of India

And there's the George Headley stand, named after George Headley.

Trevor Quirk, South African commentator

And we have just heard, although this is not the latest score from Bournemouth, that Hampshire have beaten Nottinghamshire by nine wickets.

Peter West, BBC commentator

It is important for Pakistan to take wickets if they are going to make inroads into this Australian batting line-up.

Max Walker, Australian batsman and commentator

Strangely, in slow-motion replay, the ball seemed to hang in the air even longer.

David Acfield, Essex bowler

Trevor Bailey – England Test Cricketer and Broadcaster

I don't think he expected it, and that's what caught him unawares.

Lloyd did what he achieved with that shot.

No captain with all the hindsight in the world can predict how the wicket is going to play.

On the first day Logie decided to chance his arm and it came off.

The first time you face up to a googly you're going to be in trouble if you've never faced one before.

The Port Elizabeth ground is more of a circle than an oval. It is long and square.

There are good one-day players, there are good Test players and vice versa.

This series has been swings and pendulums all the way through.

We owe some gratitude to Gatting and Lamb, who breathed some life into a corpse which had nearly expired.

Richie Benaud – Australian Test Cricketer and Broadcaster

He's not quite got hold of that one. If he had, it would have gone for nine.

   On a Justin Langer six

He's usually a good puller – but he couldn't get it up that time.

Laird has been brought in to stand in the corner of the circle.

The hallmark of a great captain is the ability to win the toss at the right time.

His throw went absolutely nowhere near where it was going.

I think the batsman's strategy will be to make runs and not get out.

This shirt is unique: there are only 200 of them.

Gatting at fine leg – that's a contradiction in terms.

There were congratulations and high sixes all round.

That slow-motion replay doesn't show how fast the ball was travelling.

Henry Blofeld – English Cricket Writer and Broadcaster

It's a catch he would have caught ninety-nine times out of a thousand.

If the tension here was a block of Cheddar cheese, you could cut it with a knife.

Flintoff starts in, his shadow beside him. Where else would it be?

In the rear, the small diminutive figure of Shoaib Mohammad, who can't be much taller than he is.

Brian Johnston – BBC Commentator

You've come over at a very appropriate time; Ray Illingworth has just relieved himself at the pavilion end.

And a sedentary seagull flies by.
   At Grace Road, Leicester

The bowler's Holding, the batsman's Willey.
   As England's Peter Willey faces up to the West Indian
   Michael Holding

As he comes in to bowl, Freddie Titmus has got two short legs, one of them square.

[Glenn] Turner looks a bit shaky and unsteady, but I think he's going to bat on ... one ball left.
   After Turner was hit in the box area by the penultimate
   ball of the match

Neil Harvey's at slip, with his legs wide apart, waiting for a tickle.

Fred Trueman – England Test Cricketer and Commentator

Anyone foolish enough to predict the outcome of this match is a fool.

I'd have looked even faster in colour.

People only call me 'Fiery' because it rhymes with Fred, just like 'Typhoon' rhymes with Tyson.

That was a tremendous six! The ball was still in the air as it went over the boundary.

That's what cricket's all about: two batsmen pitting their wits against one another.

The game's a little bit wide open again.

Unless something happens that we can't predict, I don't think a lot will happen.

We didn't have metaphors in our day. We didn't beat around the bush.

CROQUET

Chess on grass.
Anon.

It is no game for the soft of sinew and the gentle of spirit. The higher and dirtier croquet player can use the guile of a cobra and the inhumanity of a boa constrictor. Then, the general physique of a stevedore comes in handy too.
Alexander Woollcott, American writer and critic

Hurlingham rules, Croquet.
Graffito

The clunk of the ball against mallet is a lovely sound, just like ice cubes in a gin and tonic.
Sunday Times, 1987

Croquet is to be distinguished from cricket and chicken croquettes, which is a culinary term. It is ten times more exciting than tiddlywinks.
Nigel Aspinall, legendary player, 1973

CYCLING

The first cycle race probably took place as soon as the second bicycle was completed.

J. Else, *The A–Z of Cycling*, 1978

The bicycle is a curious vehicle. Its passenger is its engine.

John Howard, American pro-cyclist

The bicycle is the most civilized conveyance known to man. Other forms of transport grow daily more nightmarish. Only the bicycle remains pure in heart.

Iris Murdoch, *The Red and the Green*, 1965

When I see an adult on a bicycle, I do not despair for the future of the human race.

H. G. Wells, novelist

When man invented the bicycle he reached the peak of his attainments. Here was a machine of precision and balance for the convenience of man. And (unlike subsequent inventions for man's convenience) the more he used it, the fitter his body became. Here, for once, was a product of man's brain that was entirely beneficial to those who used it, and of no harm or irritation to others. Progress should have stopped when man invented the bicycle.

Elizabeth West, *Hovel in the Hills,* 1970

Lance Armstrong and Sheryl Crow have split up. Apparently Sheryl has met a guy who has a car.

Jay Leno, late-night host

For instance, the bicycle is the most efficient machine ever created: Converting calories into gas, a bicycle gets the equivalent of three thousand miles per gallon.

Bill Strickland, cycling journalist

The bicycle is just as good company as most husbands and, when it gets old and shabby, a woman can dispose of it and get a new one without shocking the entire community.

Ann Strong, writer, 1895

Doing the Tour [de France] again is like sex with your ex. The first five minutes is great and then you wonder why on earth you bothered.

Anonymous rider

It's bizarre, it almost seems like it's not real. To become a knight from riding your bike, it's mad.

Sir Chris Hoy, 2009

Melancholy is incompatible with bicycling.

James E. Starrs, law professor and cyclist

Until mountain biking came along, the bike scene was ruled by a small elite cadre of people who seemed allergic to enthusiasm.

Jacquie Phelan, cycling enthusiast

Get a bicycle. You will not regret it if you live.
  Mark Twain, *Taming the Bicycle*

Cycling is unique. No other sport lets you go like that – where there's only the bike left to hold you up. If you ran as hard, you'd fall over. Your legs wouldn't support you.
  Steve Johnson, cycling administrator

Talking of saddles, the first impression on climbing aboard is that it is slightly less comfortable than a meat cleaver.
  Doug Ibbotson

The sound of a car door opening in front of you is similar to the sound of a gun being cocked.
  Amy Webster, cycling writer

'I'm just off to see my brother. He's in the 6-mile bicycle race at Wembley Stadium.'
'The 6-mile bicycle race? But that finished three years ago.'
'I know, that's what I'm going to tell him.'
  Anon.

The secret to mountain biking is pretty simple. The slower you go the more likely it is you'll crash.
  Juli Furtado, American mountain biker

What do you call a cyclist who doesn't wear a helmet? An organ donor.
  David Perry

Well, it's not me. It's not me at all. It's hard work, really hard work, and it's incredibly draining. I hate it, I really hate it.

Victoria Pendleton, British Olympic gold medallist, on cycling, 2012

Some guys came here and did an air quality study. They said the breathing air in NYC is the worst breathable air in the world. They said New York's air has more chemicals in it than Lance Armstrong.

David Letterman, *Late Show*, 2012

Next week we'll be looking at the Tour de France, all those bicycles roaring through the countryside.

Andy Peebles, BBC broadcaster

DARTS

You don't have to be a beer drinker to play darts, but it helps.

Anon.

So he threw the first dart and hit a double right off – just as this bloke was putting it to his lips.

Anon.

In the World Dart Championship in 1982, Jocky Wilson missed when attempting to shake hands with an opponent.

Craig Brown, wit

I was watching sumo wrestling on the television for two hours before I realised it was darts.

Hattie Hayridge, stand-up

The world's best dart player has died at sixty-six. Cause of death was the world's worst darts player.

Craig Kilborn, comedian

I had a bash at positive thinking, yoga, transcendental meditation, even hypnotism. They only screwed me up, so now I'm back to my normal routine – a couple of lagers.

Leighton Rees, Welsh darts player

Me and a nutritionist? No, I'm too fond of chicken tikka masala.

    Adrian Lewis, English world champion darts player, 2012

One word: Bobby George.

    Colin Lloyd

He's ranked number three in Britain, number four in the world. You can't get any higher!

    John Lowe, commentator

Darts Commentator Sid Waddell's Top Seventeen Quotes

There's only one word for that – magic darts!

Jockey Wilson ... What an athlete.

When Alexander of Macedonia was thirty-three, he cried salt tears because there were no more worlds to conquer... Bristow's only twenty-seven.

That was like throwing three pickled onions into a thimble!

He's about as predictable as a wasp on speed.

Look at the man go, it's like trying to stop a water buffalo with a pea-shooter.

The atmosphere is so tense, if Elvis walked in with a portion of chips, you could hear the vinegar sizzle on them.

It's like trying to pin down a kangaroo on a trampoline.

Well, as giraffes say, you don't get no leaves unless you stick your neck out.

He looks about as happy as a penguin in a microwave.

Even Hypotenuse would have trouble working out these angles.

Phil Taylor's got the consistency of a planet ... and he's in a darts orbit!

There's no one quicker than these two tungsten tossers...

His face is sagging with tension.

The fans now, with their eyes pierced on the dart board.

He's been burning the midnight oil at both ends.

Tony Brown attacks his opponents the same way Desperate Dan attacks a cow pie.

EXERCISE

I jogged for three miles once. It was the worst three hours of my life.

Rita Rudner, stand-up

I don't think jogging is healthy, especially morning jogging. If morning joggers knew how tempting they look to motorists, they would stay at home and do sit-ups.

Rita Rudner

The trouble with jogging is that by the time you realise you're not in shape for it, it's too far to walk back.

Franklin Jones, wit

Jogging is for people who aren't intelligent enough to watch breakfast television.

Victoria Wood, actress and comedienne

Show me a man who jogs every morning and I'll show you a crumbling marriage.

Sally Poplin, humorous writer

I love jogging, except for the part after you put on your trainers.

Anon.

A friend of mine jogs ten miles every day. If you ever catch me running ten miles in a row, tell the bus driver my arm is caught in the door.

Jeff Shaw, comedian and columnist

If God had wanted us to jog on pavements, He would have given us radial toes.

Denis Norden

The first time I see a jogger smiling, I'll consider it.

Joan Rivers, comedienne

My idea of exercise is a good brisk sit.

Phyllis Diller, comedienne

Exercise is bunk. If you are healthy, you don't need it; if you are sick you shouldn't take it.

Henry Ford, car magnate

The word 'aerobics' came about when the gym instructors got together and said, 'If we're going to charge ten dollars an hour, we can't call it "jumping up and down".'

Rita Rudner

I'd lift weights, but they're so damn heavy.

Jason Love, comedian

Walking may be good exercise but did you ever see a postman as well-built as a truck driver?

Anon.

If it wasn't for the fact that the TV and the fridge are so far apart, some of us wouldn't get any exercise at all.

Joey Adams, comedian

Skipping is the best exercise for losing weight – skipping lunch, skipping dinner...

    Sally Poplin

I get all my exercise acting as a pallbearer to my friends who exercise.

    Chauncey Depew, attorney and senator

It is a fact that not once in all my life have I gone out for a walk. I have been taken out for walks; but that is another matter.

    Max Beerbohm, essayist and novelist

The only exercise I ever get it taking the cufflinks out of one shirt and putting them in another.

    Ring Lardner, sportswriter

And now for your morning exercises. Ready? Up, down, up, down, up, down, up, down. And now the other eyelid.

    Anon.

Fit? The only exercise she gets is jumping to conclusions.

    Anon.

I believe every human has a finite number of heartbeats. I don't intend to waste any of mine running around exercising.

    Neil Armstrong, astronaut

Heard the latest service for health conscious people in Beverly Hills? Valet jogging.

    Anon.

I can't believe it. This morning I jogged backwards for a mile and put on six pounds!

    Anon.

I don't exercise. What's in it for me? You've got to offer me more than my life to get me on a StairMaster, grunting for two hours. I view my body as a way of getting my head from one place to the other.

    Dave Thomas, actor and comedian

My doctor told me that exercise could add years to my life. He was right. I feel ten years older already!

    Anon.

No, I don't exercise. The way I see it, if God had meant for us to touch our toes, he would have put them further up our body.

    Anon.

I enjoy yoga. I enjoy any exercise where you get to lie down on the floor and go to sleep.

    Rita Rudner

The advantage of exercising every day is that you die healthier.

    Anon.

My favourite exercise is walking a block and a half to the corner store to buy fudge. Then I call a cab to get back home. There's never a need to overdo anything.

    Ellen DeGeneres, comedienne and host

I ran three miles today. Finally I said, 'Lady – take your purse!'
  Emo Philips, stand-up

Walking is a pleasure only when you can afford to drive if you want to.
  Anon.

In my view, ageing is natural, exercise is not. Exercise is a lot like cleaning toilets. It's something that should be done regularly but I'd like someone else to do it for me.
  Charlotte Lobb, author and stand-up

Can you stand on your head?
No, it's too high.
  Anon.

Do you take exercise after your bath?
Yes. I usually step on the soap as I get out!
  Anon.

Does your husband do any exercise?
Well, he was out last week four nights running.
  Anon.

Girl: Can you teach me to do the splits?
Instructor: How flexible are you?
Girl: Well, I can't do Fridays.
  Anon.

Whenever I read anything, it says, 'Consult your doctor before doing any exercise.' Does anybody do that? I kind of think my doctor has people coming in with serious problems. I don't think I should call him and say, 'Hi, this is Rita. I'm thinking of bending at the waist.'

Rita Rudner

FIGURE SKATING

Olympic figure skating – a sport where competitors are dressed as dinner mints.

Jeré Longman, *Philadelphia Inquirer*

Torvill and Dean were very good on the ice. But get them out on the street, they're all over the place.

Harry Hill, comedian, of Olympic ice dancers

This is a sport where you talk about sequins, earrings and plunging necklines – and you are talking about the men.

Christine Brennan, *Washington Post*

If I can't defrost this refrigerator pretty soon, I can rent it to Peggy Fleming to rehearse in.

Cher, actress and entertainer

Skating is elegant, it's safe and it's indoors. You can see some great legs on the girls and a lot of guys who'd make damn fine waiters.

Dan Jenkins, *Playboy*

It has always seemed to me hard luck on the very best ice-dancing skaters that they have to spend so much of their time whizzing along backwards, with their bottoms sticking rather undecoratively out.

Arthur Marshall, *Sunday Telegraph*, 1986

FISHING

There's a fine line between fishing and standing on the shore looking like an idiot.
    Steven Wright, stand-up comic

The formal term for a collection of fishermen is an exaggeration of anglers.
    Henry Beard, *An Angler's Dictionary*, 1983

The great thing about fishing is that it gives you something to do while you're not doing anything.
    Anon.

Oh, give me grace to catch a fish
So big that even I
When talking of it afterwards
May have no need to lie.
    Anon., 'A Fisherman's Prayer'

It has always been my private conviction that any man who pits his intelligence against a fish and loses, had it coming.
    John Steinbeck, novelist

WORK IS FOR PEOPLE WHO DON'T KNOW HOW TO FISH
    Bumper sticker, Key Biscayne, 1997

Give a man a fish and he eats for a day. Teach him to fish and you get rid of him for the whole weekend.

Zenna Schaffer, comedienne

There are too many drugs in sport but not enough in angling.

Phil Kay, comedian

I pray that I may live to fish
Until my dying day,
And when it comes to my last cast,
I then most humbly pray:
When in the Lord's great landing net,
And peacefully asleep,
That in His mercy I be judged
Big enough to keep.

Anon., 'A Fisherman's Prayer'

In literature, fishing is indeed an exhilarating sport; but, so far as my experience goes, it does not pan out when you carry the idea further.

Irvin S. Cobb, wit and newspaper columnist

Fishing is a delusion entirely surrounded by liars in old clothes.

Don Marquis, novelist, columnist and poet

We're fishing and my wife had a problem with killing the fish. I wasn't crazy with that part either, but I figured if we just wait for them to die naturally, it could take forever. Certainly till after supper.

Paul Reiser, comedian

Fishing is boring, unless you catch an actual fish, and then it is disgusting.

Dave Barry, *Miami Herald*

A fishing rod is a stick with a worm at one end and fool at the other.

Samuel Johnson, wit

FOOTBALL

Five days shalt thou labour, as the Bible says. The seventh day is the Lord thy God's. The sixth day is for football.

Anthony Burgess, novelist

I would have thought that the knowledge that you are going to be leapt upon by half-a-dozen congratulatory, but sweaty, teammates would be inducement not to score a goal.

Arthur Marshall, writer

Radio football is football reduced to its lowest common denominator. Shorn of the game's aesthetic pleasures, or the comfort of a crowd that feels the same way as you, or the sense of security that you get when you see that your defenders and goalkeeper are more or less where they should be, all that is left is naked fear.

Nick Hornby, *Fever Pitch*, 1992

A player who conjugates a verb in the first person singular cannot be part of the squad, he has to conjugate the verb in the first person plural. We. We want to conquer. We are going to conquer. Using the word 'I' when you're in a group makes things complicated.

Vanderlei Luxemburgo, Brazilian football manager, 1999

Bobby Robson's natural expression is that of a man who fears he may have left the gas on.

David Lacey, sportswriter

I fell in love with football as I would later fall in love with women: suddenly, uncritically, giving no thought to the pain it would bring.

Nick Hornby, novelist

I loathed the game, and since I could see no pleasure or usefulness in it, it was very difficult for me to show courage at it. Football, it seemed to me, is not really played for the pleasure of kicking a ball about, but is a species of fighting.

George Orwell, writer

One minute I was painting the lounge, the next I'm being asked to manage a Championship side. My wife will have to finish the glossing.

Ian Holloway, manager of Blackpool

You're not a real manager unless you've been sacked.

Malcolm Allison, player, manager and pundit

The long ball down the middle is like pouring beer down the toilet. It cuts out the middleman.

Jack Charlton, Leeds United and England international

A real Irish football fan is one who knows the true nationality of every player on the Republic of Ireland team.

Jack Charlton, former Republic of Ireland manager

Emile Heskey has the turning circle of a 747.

Anon.

Manchester City are the only team in the world to get the crowd to autograph the ball after the game.
Bernard Manning, comedian

A goalkeeper is a goalkeeper because he can't play football.
Ruud Gullit, Dutch player and manager

When God gave him this enormous footballing talent, he took his brain out at the same time to equal it up.
Tony Banks, politician and broadcaster, of Paul Gascoigne

A teabag stays in the cup longer.
Anon., of any team knocked out in the first round.

Dracula is more comfortable with crosses.
Anon., of many goalkeepers

They call him Cinderella because he's always late for the ball.
Anon., of many goalkeepers

If you needed someone to take a penalty kick to save your life, Chris Waddle, with his hunched shoulders and lethargic air, would rank just below Long John Silver.
Anon.

At Glasgow Rangers I was third choice left-back behind an amputee and a Catholic.
Craig Brown, Scottish player and manager

They've had to replace the new executive boxes at West Brom because they were pointed in the wrong direction. They were facing the pitch!
Anon.

That's great, tell him he's Pele and get him back on.
John Lambie, Partick Thistle manager, when told a
concussed striker didn't know who he was

In football everything is complicated by the presence of the
opposite team.
Jean-Paul Sartre, French writer

He's got one of the least demanding jobs in the country.
He's the official scorer for Plymouth Argyle.
Anon.

The Glaswegian definition of an atheist: a bloke who goes
to a Rangers–Celtic match to watch the football.
Sandy Strang, Scottish raconteur

The goalkeeper is the jewel in the crown and getting at him
should be almost impossible. It's the biggest sin in football
to make him do any work.
George Graham, Arsenal player and manager

Clive is a football connoisseur and an Arsenal fan.
I've never quite seen the connection myself, but...
Anon.

As far as his team's concerned, he's the eternal optimist. He
says they can still get promotion if they win eleven out of
their last four games.
Anon.

For a minute we were in with a great chance. Then the
game started.
Anon.

He's got the brains of a rocking horse.
>   Dave Bassett, manager, of Sheffield United's goalkeeper,
>   Simon Tracey

He cannot kick with his left foot. He cannot head a ball. He cannot tackle and he doesn't score many goals. Apart from that, he's all right.
>   George Best, former Manchester United player, of David
>   Beckham

For years I thought the club's name was Partick Thistle Nil.
>   Billy Connolly, comedian

He's the moaningest Minnie I've ever known.
>   John Bond of fellow manager Kenny Dalglish

There's more meat on a toothpick.
>   Alan Birchenall, Leicester City player, of Robbie Savage

Filippo Inzaghi must have been born offside.
>   Sir Alex Ferguson, Manchester United manager, of the AC
>   Milan goalscorer

He needed five stitches – three in the first half and two at the interval when his brain started to seep though.
>   Sir Alex Ferguson, of Steve Bruce

Part of the problem is Eric won't tackle. He couldn't tackle a fish supper.
>   Sir Alex Ferguson, of his player, Eric Cantona

To the world at large he resembles an irascible pensioner who has watched too many episodes of *The Sopranos*.
>   Patrick Collins, sportswriter, of Alex Ferguson

I doubt if Sven-Göran Eriksson has even heard of Ian Wright. If only the rest of us could say the same.

Patrick Collins

Bellamy was no more than a bovine, charmless, virtually friendless clown. His achievements are slender, his notoriety immense. He is the kind of player who attracts fines and enemies in equal measure, the kind whose natural expression wavers between scowl and sneer, the kind, in short, who gives professional footballers the reputation they now enjoy.

Patrick Collins, of Craig Bellamy

There are torch-carrying search parties out looking for the bundle of promise that used to be Shaun Wright-Phillips.

Paul Hayward, sportswriter, *Daily Mail*

Poor Fulham, with no real method up front, resembled a fire engine hurrying to the wrong fire.

Geoffrey Green, sportswriter

I try to keep fit. I had a new hip put in two and a half years ago and it's made a big difference to my life. I did Pilates the other day and it was hilarious. All this 'breathe in and stabilise' stuff. The instructor never told us to breathe out again, so for two minutes I was holding my breath. Nearly killed myself.

Gordon Strachan, Middlesbrough manager, on coping with the pressure

He started watching Arsenal after his doctor advised him to avoid excitement.

Anon.

They're not a great team. In fact, they're so starved of success that they do a lap of honour every time they get a corner.

Anon.

Snow White arrived home one evening to find her house destroyed by fire. She was doubly worried because she'd left all seven dwarfs asleep inside. As she scrambled among the wreckage, frantically calling their names, suddenly she heard the cry: 'Tottenham for the Cup!'

'Thank goodness,' sobbed Snow White. 'At least Dopey's still alive.'

Anon.

Pass a ball? He'd have trouble passing wind.

Alf Ramsey, England manager, of Dutch international
Piet Fransen

Kevin Keegan is not fit to lace George Best's drinks.

John Roberts, Welsh international

... daft as a brush.

Sir Bobby Robson, England manager, of his player
Paul Gascoigne

José Mourinho recently turned down the post of Pope when he heard it was something in the way of an assistant position.

Harry Pearson, columnist

Due to recent riots, an Italian soccer league is forcing teams to play games with no fans in the stadium. Which, coincidentally, is how soccer games are played here in America.

Conan O'Brien, late-night host

Birmingham City – you lose some, you draw some.
  Jasper Carrott, English comedian

Burglars recently broke into Torquay United's ground and
stole the entire contents of the trophy room.
  Police are looking for a man with a blue and white carpet.
  Anon.

Ally MacLeod thinks that tactics are a new kind of
peppermint.
  Billy Connolly, comedian, on the Scotland manager

Football is all very well as a game for rough girls, but it is
hardly suitable for delicate boys.
  Oscar Wilde, attrib.

I said, 'What is the matter with you Tom, what's the trou-
ble?' He said, 'I've got a bad back,' so I told him, I said,
'There's no need to worry about that – our team's got two.'
  Robb Wilton, BBC Light Programme, 1952

I've told the players we need to win so that I can have the
cash to buy some new ones.
  Chris Turner, Peterborough manager, before League Cup
  quarter-final, 1992

I love Liverpool so much that if I caught one of their players
in bed with my missus, I'd tiptoe downstairs and make him
a cup of tea.
  Keen fan

Last time we got a penalty away from home, Christ was still
a carpenter.
  Lennie Lawrence, manager

I promised I would take Rotherham out of the Second
Division. I did – into the Third Division.
  Tommy Docherty, Scottish player and manager

They beat us 5–0 – and we were lucky to score nil.
  Anon.

I went down to pass on some technical information to the
team – like the fact that the game had started.
  Ron Atkinson, Aston Villa's manager, explaining why he
  had taken his seat at the touchline earlier than usual during
  a home defeat against Sheffield United

QUEEN IN BRAWL AT PALACE.
  Guardian headline after Gerry Queen was sent off as
  Crystal Palace played Arsenal

Don't try it at home, unless you're on a bouncy castle.
  Jamie Redknapp, player and pundit, referring to Zlatan
  Ibrahimovic's stunning 'bicycle-kick' goal for Sweden
  against England, 2012

The shape was good, the passing was good, the movement
was good. The result was crap.
  Roy Hodgson, manager of West Brom, on their game
  against Spurs

I'm going to pick myself, not take myself off, be the captain,
take throw-ins, everything.
  Nick Barmby, outlining his plans for being player-manager
  at Hull

It's clash of the titans. A rubbish home record against a rubbish away record so we'll see what goes on.

Mick McCarthy, Wolves manager, before playing Swansea

You see grown men like Joey Barton dropping to the floor. They must do football in the morning and acting in the afternoon. If a bloke did that in rugby he'd have twenty blokes in the tunnel waiting for him.

Sam Tomkins, full-back of rugby league Wigan

We've seen a very nice airport.

Robin van Persie, footballer, asked for his initial impressions of Malaysia minutes after landing

The cat is in the sack, but the sack is not closed. The cat is in it, but it's open – and it's a wild cat.

Giovanni Trapattoni, Italian football coach

As long as my family don't boo me when I walk through the door, I couldn't care less!

Michael Owen, reacting to being booed by Newcastle fans

Running tracks and football grounds sit together about as well as putting a swimming pool on Centre Court.

Harry Redknapp, Tottenham manager, 2011

If that had happened in our day, Billy Bonds would have put him up against a wall, given him a right hook and knocked his tooth out for him!

Phil Parkes, former West Ham goalkeeper of then West Ham player, Frenchman Frédéric Piquionne, who was taking time off to visit the dentist

You don't see us jumping in the referee's face when something goes wrong and waving our fingers at him trying to get the other player on the other side of the fairway carded. You don't see us missing a putt and diving.

  Lee Westwood, English golfer, on the differences between
  golfers and footballers

I helped him a bit with his crosses today. He needs to get his foot around the ball a bit. If he can do that, I think he has a future in the game.

  Harry Redknapp, reflecting on David Beckham training
  with Spurs in 2011

It makes me want to snap my cast off and run up there and find him.

  Jamie Mackie, QPR striker after Blackburn's El Hadji
  Diouf taunted him about his broken leg

I was going to call him a sewer rat but that might be insulting to sewer rats.

  Neil Warnock, QPR manager, attacking El Hadji Diouf for
  the same incident

Ferguson has a left foot you could peel oranges with.

  Alan Pardew, Newcastle manager on their academy player
  Shane Ferguson

He made a comment like: 'It's all getting messy' ... this somehow translated into: 'Get Messi'.

  Garry Cook, former Manchester City chief, on how the
  club ended up making a £30 million bid for Leo Messi

There's about as much chance of re-signing DJ Campbell as there is of me wearing high heels and calling myself Sheila.

Ian Holloway, on the chances of DJ Campbell returning to Blackpool

Leighton James is very deceptive. He's even slower than he looks.

Tommy Docherty, on the Welsh international winger

Everyone knows that for Manchester United to get a penalty we need a certificate from the Pope and a personal letter from the Queen.

Sir Alex Ferguson

Maybe Napoleon was wrong when he said we were a nation of shopkeepers... Today England looked like a nation of goalkeepers.

Tom Stoppard, *Professional Foul*, BBC TV, 1977

The centre forward said, 'It was an open goal – but I put it straight over the crossbar! I could kick myself!' And the manager said, 'I wouldn't bother, you'd probably miss!'

Fred Metcalf for David Frost, *TV-am*, 1984

[Italian defensive midfielder] Tardelli's been responsible for more scar tissue than the surgeons of Harefield Hospital.

Jimmy Greaves, ITV World Cup Panel, 1982

When Charlie Cooke sold you a dummy, you had to pay to get back into the ground.

Jim Baxter, Scottish international, on his teammate

Come on you blue two-tone hoops with red and white trim and a little emblem on the sleeve and the manufacturer's logo and the sponsor's name across the chest!

Mike Ticher, fan

The secret of football is to equalise before the opposition scores.

Danny Blanchflower, footballer, manager and journalist

A million quid for Mark Hateley? But he can't even trap a dead rat!

Stan Bowles, of a fellow pro

Football hooligans? Well, there are the ninety-two club chairmen, for a start.

Brian Clough, manager, Nottingham Forest

Who wants to be a football manager? Well, people like me who are too old to play, too poor to be a director and too much in love with the game to be an agent.

Steve Coppell, former Crystal Palace manager

Last Saturday I watched a really cracking football match. One of those matches you walk home from thinking, 'Yes, that is what soccer is all about.' Fourteen fouls in the first ten minutes, fists flung, throats elbowed, eyes poked, shins hacked, shirts ripped, hair pulled, enough ballistic saliva to fill a trainer's bucket, and a richer variety of air-blueing oaths, I'll wager, than Mary Whitehouse has been able to net in a lifetime's trawling.

Utterly professional. Totally committed. Prodigiously physical. Impressively cynical. Above all, unstintingly competitive, and not a player on the field over twelve years old.

Alan Coren

You know you've become obsessed with football when you video games of Subbuteo for post-game analysis.

Anon.

I'm not saying my husband's becoming obsessed with football but he's begun to refer to our sofa as 'the dugout'.

Anon.

He had a bandage on his head. Perhaps one of his eyelashes had fallen out.

George Graham, of Tomas Brolin, Swedish international

Football is an art more central to our culture than anything the Arts Council deigns to recognise.

Germaine Greer, *The Independent*, 1996

I never went in for aerial challenges at Liverpool. You lose 150 brain cells every time you head a ball. I used to make Mark Lawrenson do all the heading. You have to delegate. It's a captain's prerogative.

Alan Hansen, player and commentator

The natural state of the football fan is bitter disappointment, no matter what the score.

Nick Hornby, *Fever Pitch*, 1992

The first half was the sort of thing you'd rather watch on Ceefax.

Gary Lineker, after watching Wimbledon play in 1993

To say that these men paid their shillings to watch twenty-two hirelings kick a ball is merely to say that a violin is wood and catgut, that *Hamlet* is so much paper and ink. For a shilling the Bruddersford United AFC offered you Conflict and Art.

  J. B. Priestley, *Good Companions*, 1929

Ossie Ardiles was the difference. It was like trying to tackle dust.

  Joe Royle, after his Oldham side was knocked out of the
  FA Cup by Tottenham in January 1988

The rules of soccer are simple. Basically it is this: if it moves, kick it. If it doesn't move, kick it until it does.

  Phil Woosnam, on forming the North American Soccer
  League, 1974

Our club manager won't stand for any nonsense. Last Saturday he caught a couple of fans climbing over the stadium wall. He was furious. He grabbed them by the collars and said, 'Now you just get back in there and watch the game till it finishes!'

  Anon.

It's an incredible rise to stardom. At seventeen you're more likely to get a call from Michael Jackson than Sven-Göran Eriksson.

  Gordon Strachan, referring to Wayne Rooney

I spent 90 per cent of my money on women, drink and fast cars. The rest I wasted!

  George Best

Raul, man, he's like a Twinkie. He would survive a nuclear war.

Ray Hudson, player and commentator

We'll still be happy if we lose. The game's on at the same time as the Beer Festival.

Cork City manager Noel O'Mahoney before a game in Munich

If you stand still there is only one way to go, and that's backwards.

Peter Shilton, England goalkeeper

In 1978, in between Manchester City winning one game and their next win, there had been three Popes.

Frank Skinner, British comedian

Statistics are like miniskirts – they give you good ideas but hide the important things.

Ebbe Skovdahl, Danish football manager

When Manchester United are at their best I am close to orgasm.

Gianluca Vialli, Italian player and manager

I thought you said he eats, drinks and sleeps football. *He does, he just can't play it.*

Anon.

There are only two types of managers. Those who've just been sacked and those who are going to be sacked.

Ben Philip, sporting wit

The referee was booking everyone. I thought he was filling in his lottery numbers.

Ian Wright, player and commentator

If Stan Bowles could pass a betting shop like he can pass a ball, he'd have no worries at all.

Ernie Tagg, player and manager, Crewe Alexandra

Norman Hunter doesn't tackle opponents so much as break them down for resale as scrap.

Julie Welch, sportswriter

Even Jesus Christ wasn't liked by everyone. What hope is there for me?

José Mourinho, Internazionale manager, 2009

My secret is adapting to the country I am in. Here I eat roast beef and Yorkshire pudding.

Arsène Wenger, Arsenal manager

I want to help other clubs. I speak my mind and other chairmen should too. In fact, they can come and have lunch with me at Harrods, where I can serve them stags' testicles from my Scottish estate. We all need big balls in this business.

Mohamed Al Fayed, chairman of Fulham and owner
of Harrods

Football Songs and Chants:

You're not yodelling, you're not yodelling, you're not yodelling any more

Newcastle fans after scoring away at FC Zurich

When you're sat in row Z, and the ball hits your head, that's
Zamora, that's Zamora
> Fulham fans on goal-shy Bobby Zamora

I can't read and I can't write
But that don't really matter
'Cos I comes from the West Country
And I can drive a tractor!
> Exeter City chant

Inger-land, Inger-land, Inger-land
Inger-land, Inger-land, Inger-land
Inger-land, Inger-land, Inger-land
Inger-land
INGER LAND
> England chant – to be repeated for most of the match

Sing when you're whaling
You only sing when you're whaling
> Sung by the Scotland fans when their team played Norway
> in the 1998 World Cup finals

He flies through the air with the greatest of ease
He never got touched, but he's down on his knees
> Spurs chant in honour of frequent diver Jurgen Klinsmann

Down with pneumonia. We're going down with pneumonia!
> Rain-soaked Charlton fans behind the uncovered goal at
> Yeovil's Huish Park, 2009

We're all mad, we're insane,
We eat Mars bars on the train.
> Leyton Orient supporters

One nil to the Cockney Boys
One nil to the Cockney Boys
One nil to the Cockney Boys!
REPEAT.
  West Ham chant (Best available)

Brian Clough – Legendary Nottingham Forest Manager

He couldn't trap a landmine.
  Of Gary Megson, player and coach

Trevor Brooking floats like a butterfly – and stings like one.

I told Eddie Gray that, with his injury record, if he'd been a racehorse they'd have had him shot.

Dutch goalkeepers are protected to a ridiculous extent. The only time they are in danger of physical contact is when they go into a red-light district.

Brian Clough's record speaks for itself. If it can get a word in.
  Cris Freddi, British author

Tommy Docherty – Scottish Player, and Manager of Thirteen Clubs

I've had more clubs than Jack Nicklaus!

The ideal board of directors should be made up of three men: two dead and the other dying.

Wimbledon have as much charm as a broken beer bottle.

I just opened the trophy cabinet. Two Japanese prisoners of war jumped out.

At Wolves

There are three types of OXO cubes. Light brown for chicken stock, dark brown for beef stock, and light blue for laughing stock.

Of Manchester City

Tony Hateley had it all. The only thing he lacked was ability.

I wouldn't only not sign him, I wouldn't let him in the ground.

Of Vinnie Jones

Bill Shankly – Legendary Liverpool Manager

This city has two great football teams – Liverpool and Liverpool reserves.

Some people think football is a matter of life and death. I don't like that attitude. I can assure them it is much more serious than that.

Look laddie, if you're in the penalty area and aren't quite sure what to do with the ball, just stick it in the net and we'll discuss all your options afterwards.

Professional footballers should have more sense than to consider marrying during the season. Anybody who does isn't behaving professionally as far as I'm concerned.

If Everton were playing down at the bottom of my garden, I'd draw the curtains.

Matt has got a bad back. I tell you it's two bad backs! And not much of a midfield either.

Of Manchester United manager Matt Busby

We murdered them nil-all.

The difference between Everton and the *Queen Mary* is that Everton carry more passengers.

When I've got nothing better to do, I look down the league table to see how Everton are getting along.

Ron Atkinson – Player, Manager and Pundit

He dribbles a lot and the opposition don't like it – you can see it all over their faces.

I think that the action replay showed it to be worse than it actually was.

They've picked their heads up off the ground and they now have a lot to carry on their shoulders.

Moreno thought that the full-back was gonna come up behind and give him one really hard.

0–0 is a big score!

Yes, Woodcock would have scored but his shot was just too perfect.

The Spaniards have been reduced to aiming aimless balls into the box.

I would not say he is the best left-winger in the Premiership, but there are none better.

Well, Clive, it's all about the two 'M's. Movement and Positioning.

Well, either side could win it, or it could be a draw.

Bryon Butler – BBC Radio Commentator

52,000 people here at Maine Road tonight but, my good-ness me, it seems like 50,000.

That now means that from the British point of view, Anderlecht lead 3–2.

United have a very experienced bench which they may want to play to turn the tide of the match.

And Bailey comes out to save, immediately there is a whole wasp's nest of blue shirts swarming around him.

And so now the fair, long hair of Adrian Heath has been thrown into action.

Butcher goes forward as Ipswich throw their last trump card into the fire.

And the second goal was a blueprint of the first.

He put it just where he meant it and it passed the Luxembourg goal post by eighteen inches.

Wilkins sends an inch perfect pass to no one in particular.

Wolves keeper John Burridge has consciously modelled himself on the great Peter Shilton, same sort of hair style.

David Coleman – BBC Commentator

Nottingham Forest are having a bad run. They've lost six matches in a row now without winning.

If that had gone in, it would have been a goal.

And now International Soccer Special, Manchester United vs. Southampton.

Don't tell those coming in now the result of that fantastic match. Now let's have another look at Italy's winning goal.

In fact that's Swindon's first win of any kind in nine matches.

On this 101st FA Cup Final day, there are just two teams left.

The pace of this match is really accelerating, by which I mean it is getting faster all the time.

For those of you watching who haven't TV sets, live commentary is on Radio Two.

The ball has broken 50–50 for Keegan.

Both of the Villa scorers – Withe and Mortimer – were born in Liverpool, as was the Villa manager, Ron Saunders, who was born in Birkenhead.

Manchester United are buzzing around the goalmouth like a lot of red bottles.

Kevin Keegan – Player, Manager and Pundit

Argentina are the second-best team in the world and there's no higher praise than that.

The ref was vertically 15 yards away.

Chile have three options – they could win or they could lose.

I came to Nantes two years ago and it's much the same today, except that it's completely different.

England has the best fans in the world and Scotland's fans are second-to-none.

I'll never play at Wembley again, unless I play at Wembley again.

The Germans only have one player under twenty-two, and he's twenty-three!

The tide is very much in our court now.

I'd love to be a mole on the wall in the Liverpool dressing room at half-time.

Brian Moore – ITV Commentator

And now we have the formalities over, we'll have the National Anthems.

The whole team stopped as one man, but Arkwright in particular.

Mark Ward has only got size-five boots but he sure packs a hell of a punch with them.

Souness's football brain working at a hundred miles an hour there.

Wayne Clarke, one of the famous Clarke family, and he's one of them, of course.

You can see how O'Leary is absolutely racked with pain, and realises it.

Newcastle, of course, unbeaten in their last five wins.

GAFFES AND BLOOPERS

We must have had 99 per cent of the game. It was the other 3 per cent that cost us the match.
  Ruud Gullit

Julian Dicks is everywhere. It's like they've got eleven Dicks on the field.
  Metro Radio football reporter

The midfield picks itself: Beckham, Scholes, Gerrard and A. N. Other.

Phil Neal, player, manager and pundit

Batistuta gets most of his goals with the ball.

Ian St John, ITV football commentator

If history repeats itself, I should think we can expect the same thing again.

Terry Venables, England football manager and pundit

I don't like to see players tossed off needlessly.

Andy Gray, player and pundit

When you are 4–0 up you should never lose 7–1.

Lawrie McMenemy, manager of Southampton

The beauty of Cup football is that Jack always has a chance of beating Goliath.

Terry Butcher, player and manager

And Farmer has now scored nineteen goals, exactly double the number he scored last season.

Garry Lyon, Australian football commentator

Winning doesn't really matter as long as you win.

Vinnie Jones, Welsh player and pundit

Despite the rain, it's still raining here at Old Trafford.

Jimmy Hill, BBC commentator

Is the Pope Catholic? No, I'm serious, is he? I really need to know.

> David Beckham, when asked if he might be moving to
> AS Roma

Diego Maradona – a flawed genius who has now become a genius who is flawed.

> Bob Wilson, goalkeeper and pundit

The underdogs will start favourites for this match.

> Anthony Hudson, Australian football commentator

And Sheffield Wednesday the winners 2–0, leaving the Anfield crowd brainwashed.

> Stuart Hall, BBC commentator

And Watford acknowledge the support of the crowd, indeed of the crowd that supported them.

> Barry Davies, BBC commentator

Anything from 1–0 to 2–0 would be a nice result.

> Sir Bobby Robson

At least it was a victory and at least we won.

> Bobby Moore, West Ham and England captain

But as you know, the result for City is not as bad as it sounds on paper.

> Steve McIlwain

I don't hold water with that theory.

Ron Greenwood, West Ham and England manager and
TV pundit

I think Charlie George was one of Arsenal's all-time great players. A lot of people might not agree with that, but I personally do.

Jimmy Greaves, England player and pundit

In the Scottish Cup you only get one crack at the cherry against Rangers or Celtic.

Tom Ferrie, Scottish broadcaster

It slid away from his left boot which was poised with the trigger cocked.

Barry Davies

It's now 4–3 to Oldham, the goals are going in like dominoes.

Piccadilly Radio, Manchester

Plenty of goals in Divisions 3 and 4 today. Darlington nil, Hereford nil.

BBC Radio 2

The margin is very marginal.

Sir Bobby Robson

There are still hundreds of question marks to be answered.

Jimmy Armfield, player, manager and BBC pundit

There were two second division matches last night, both in the second division.

Dominic Allen, broadcaster

They have more ability in the middle of the field in terms of ability.

Jimmy Armfield

We have been saying this, both pre-season and before the season started.

Len Ashurst, player and manager

Wembley Way is beginning to be blocked with people in terms of red and blue.

Alan Jackson, top scorer for Bury

At the end of the day, the Arsenal fans demand that we put eleven players on the pitch.

Don Howe, Arsenal manager

Believe it or not, goals can change a game.

Mick Channon, player and pundit

Halifax against Spurs, the original David against Goliath confrontation.

John Helm, ITV commentator

He hit the post, and after the game people will say, well, he hit the post.

Jimmy Greaves

I think you and the referee were in a minority of one, Billy.

Jimmy Armfield

Ian Durrant has grown both physically and metaphorically in the close season.

Jock Wallace, Scottish player and Rangers manager

Ian Rush unleashed his left foot and it hit the back of the net.

Mike England, Welsh player and manager

Ian Rush, deadly ten times out of ten, but that wasn't one of them.

Peter Jones, Welsh BBC commentator

It was a fair decision, the penalty, even though it was debatable whether it was inside or outside the box.

Bobby Charlton, former Manchester United and England player

It will be a shame if either side loses, and that applies to both sides.

Jock Brown, Scottish football commentator

Manchester United have got the bull between the horns now.

Billy McNeill, Scottish player and manager

Newport 0, Wrexham 1. Well done the Welsh there.

BBC Radio 2

'Numero Eins', as they say in Germany.

Peter Jones

Peter Shilton conceded five, you don't get many of those to the dozen.

Des Lynam, BBC radio and TV presenter

Portsmouth are at Huddersfield, which is always away.
    Jimmy Greaves

So often the pendulum continues to swing with the side that
has just pulled themselves out of the hole.
    Tony Gubba, journalist and commentator

That goal surprised most people, least of all myself.
    Garth Crooks, player and commentator

The red hair of John Brown on the bench there.
    Archie Macpherson, Scottish commentator and author

The run of the ball is not in our court at the moment.
    Phil Neal

This is a one-off occasion and you can't get any bigger
occasion than that.
    Bryan Robson, player and manager

We go into the second half with United 1–0 up, so the game
is perfectly balanced.
    Peter Jones

Well actually we got the winner up there with three minutes
to go, but then they equalised.
    Ian McNail, Scottish player

Well Kerry, you're nineteen and you're a lot older than a lot
of people younger than yourself.
    Mike Gray, player and pundit

Well Terry, can you tell us where you are in the league, how far are you ahead of the second team?

Ian St John

Yes, he is not unused to playing in midfield, but at the same time he's not used to playing there either.

Emlyn Hughes, Liverpool and England captain and pundit

You'll be hoping that this run of injuries will stop earlier than it started.

Andrew Gidley, reporter

£5.3 million is a large loaf to be throwing away before a ball's been kicked.

Jimmy Greaves

A win tonight is the minimum City must achieve.

Alan Parry, Sky Sports commentator

And Meade had a hat-trick. He scored two goals.

Richard Whitmore, BBC newsreader

Billy Gilbert hit a kamikaze back pass which Justin Fashanu pounced on like a black Frank Bruno.

Ian Darke, commentator

Bryan Robson, well, he does what he does and his future is in the future.

Ron Greenwood

Chesterfield 1, Chester 1. Another score draw in the local derby.

Des Lynam

Everything in our favour was against us.

   Danny Blanchflower, Northern Ireland and Spurs player
   and journalist

Football is a game of skill, we kicked them a bit and they
kicked us a bit.

   Graham Roberts, player, manager and international coach

His strengths were my weaknesses and my weaknesses were
his strengths.

   John Bond, West Ham player and Norwich City manager

I can't promise anything but I can promise 100%.

   Paul Power, Manchester City player

I don't blame individuals, Elton, I blame myself.

   Joe Royle

I think everyone in the stadium went home happy, except
all those people in Romania.

   Ron Greenwood

I'm afraid that Francis this season has been suffering from
a panacea of injury.

   Dale Barnes, Canadian football administrator

I'm not superstitious or anything like that, but I'll just hope
we'll play our best and put it in the lap of the gods.

   Terry Neill, Northern Ireland player and manager

In Scotland football hooliganism has been met by banning alcohol from grounds but in England this solution has been circumnavigated.

Wallace Mercer, Heart of Midlothian chairman

It really needed the blink of an eyelid, otherwise you would have missed it.

Peter Jones

It was a good match, which could have gone either way and very nearly did.

Jim Sherwin, Irish commentator

It's a renaissance, or put more simply, some you win, some you lose.

Des Lynam

John Lyall, very much a claret and blue man, from his stocking feet to his hair.

Peter Jones

Manchester United are looking to Frank Stapleton to pull some magic out of the fire.

Jimmy Hill

McCarthy shakes his head in agreement with the referee.

Martin Tyler, TV commentator and coach

Northern Ireland were in white, which was quite appropriate because three inches of snow had to be cleared from the pitch before kick-off.

John Motson, BBC radio and TV commentator

Oh, he had an eternity to play that ball, but he took too long over it.

Martin Tyler

Once again it was Gough who stood firm for Scotland in the air.

Jock Brown

Peter Weir has just shrugged off an ankle injury.

Jock Brown

Players win games and players lose games, it's all about players really.

Bobby Ferguson, Scottish footballer

Spurs, one of the in-form teams of the moment with successive wins are almost as impressive as Queens Park Rangers with five.

Bob Wilson

Stevens got to the line, crossed the ball and Lineker wrapped it all up with his head.

Ralph Dellor, reporter and commentator

The boys' feet have been up in the clouds since the win.

Alan Buckley, English footballer and manager

The dice are stacked against them.

Theo Foley, Exeter City player and Arsenal coach

The scoreline didn't really reflect the outcome.

Tony Gubba

There is no change in the top six of Division 2, except that Leeds have moved into the top six.

Fred Dinenage, English TV newsreader

Walsall have given City more than one anxious moment amongst many anxious moments.

Denis Law, Manchester United and Scotland player
and pundit

Well, clearly, Graeme, it all went according to plan. What was the plan exactly?

Elton Welsby, ITV presenter

Well, he had two stabs at the cherry.

Alan Green, BBC Radio commentator

We've got nothing to lose, and there's no point losing this game.

Sir Bobby Robson

Whoever wins today will win the championship no matter who wins.

Denis Law

... and now the Northern Ireland manager, Billy Bingham, will have to put his thinking boots on.

BBC Radio

A few question marks are being asked in the Honduran defence.

Alan Green

Again Mariner and Butcher are trying to work the oracle on the near post.

Martin Tyler

And at the end of the season you can only do as well as what you have done.

Bryan Robson

And Ritchie has now scored eleven goals, exactly double the number he scored last season.

Alan Parry

... and then there was Johan Cruyff, who at thirty-five has added a whole new meaning to *anno domini*.

Archie Macpherson

And Wigan Athletic are certain to be promoted barring a mathematical tragedy.

Tony Gubba

... and with eight minutes left the game could be won or lost in the next five or ten minutes.

Jimmy Armfield

Ardiles always says, 'If you're confident you're always totally different to the player that's lacking confidence.'

Keith Burkinshaw, player and manager

Arsenal, with Petrović anonymous.

David Davies, commentator and football administrator

At the end of the day, it's all about what's on the shelf at the end of the year.

Steve Coppell, England player and manager

Being given chances, and not taking them. That's what life is all about.

Ron Greenwood

But the ball was going all the way, right away, eventually.

Archie Macpherson

Bryon Butler: You'd obviously made up your mind to play both Stein and Walsh?
Bobby Robson: Yes, I thought that individually and as a pair, they'd do better together.

Dickie Davies: What's he going to be telling his team at half-time, Denis?
Denis Law: He'll be telling them that there are forty-five minutes left to play.

Even when you're dead you shouldn't lie down and let yourself be buried.

Gordon Lee, player and manager

Football's all about ninety minutes.

Glenn Hoddle, Spurs and England midfielder

Football's football, if that weren't the case it wouldn't be the game that it is.

Garth Crooks

Great goal by Moss, straight into the textbook.

Gerry Harrison, ITV commentator

He hit that one like an arrow.

Alan Parry

Here's Brian Flynn. His official height is 5 feet 5 and he doesn't look much taller than that.
    Alan Green

He's marked his entrance with an error of some momentum.
    Barry Davies

Hodge scored for Forest after only twenty-two seconds, totally against the run of play.
    Peter Lorenzo, ITV presenter

I am a firm believer that if you score one goal the other team have to score two to win.
    Howard Wilkinson, English player and manager

I can't see us getting beat now, once we get our tails in front.
    Jim Platt, Northern Ireland goalkeeper

I do want to play the long ball and I do not want to play the short ball. I think long and short balls is what football is all about.
    Sir Bobby Robson

I don't know if that result's enough to lift Birmingham off the bottom of the table, although it'll certainly take them above Sunderland.
    Mike Ingham, BBC football correspondent

I don't really believe in targets, because my next target is to beat Stoke City.
    Ron Wylie, Scottish player, coach and manager

I felt a lump in my mouth as the ball went in.
   Terry Venables

I predicted in August Celtic would reach the final. On the
eve of the final I stand by that prediction.
James Sanderson, Scottish football journalist
Ian St John: Is he speaking to you yet?
Jimmy Greaves: Not yet, but I hope to be incommunicado
with him in a very short space of time.

I'd have to be Superman to do some of the things I'm
supposed to have done. I've been at six different places at
six different times.
   George Best

I'd like to have seen Tony Morley left on as a down and
out winger.
   Jimmy Armfield

If England had scored in the first half, I think the young legs
would have found younger hearts inside them.
   Jimmy Armfield

If you had to name one particular person to blame it would
have to be one of the players.
   Theo Foley

I'm not going to make it a target but it's something to
aim for.
   Steve Coppell, England player and manager

Interviewer: In your new book, Pat, you've devoted a whole chapter to Jimmy Greaves.

Pat Jennings: Yes that's right, well what can you say about Jimmy?

It feels like winning the cup final, if that's what it feels like.
> Graham Hawkins, player and manager

It is a cup final and the one who wins it goes through.
> Jimmy Hill

It's a game of two teams.
> Peter Brackley, Channel 4 commentator

It's always very satisfying to beat Arsenal, as indeed Arsenal would admit.
> Peter Jones

John Bond has brought in a young left-sided midfield player, who, I guess, will play on the left side of midfield.
> Jimmy Armfield

Kicked wide of the goal with such precision.
> Des Lynam

Mabbutt has now played seven consecutive games for England, this is his seventh.
> Martin Tyler

Most of the people who can remember when we were a great club are dead.
> Notts County chairman

Not the first half you might have expected, even though the score might suggest that it was.

John Motson

Obviously for Scunthorpe it would be a nice scalp to put Wimbledon on their bottoms.

Dave Bassett, player, manager and pundit

One of Asa's great qualities is not scoring goals.

Roy Small, Scottish manager, of international midfielder
Asa Hartford

Queen's Park against Forfar, you can't get more romantic than that.

Archie Macpherson, Scottish commentator and author

Quiroga touches it away. Nothing he doesn't do that isn't spectacular.

Gerry Harrison, ITV commentator, of Argentinian
international Ramon Quiroga

Real possession football, this. And Zico's lost it.

John Helm, ITV commentator, of Brazilian international

So it means that, mathematically, Southampton have fifty-eight points.

Peter Jones

So that's 1–0, sounds like the score at Boundary Park where of course it's 2–2.

Jack Wainwright, Radio Leeds commentator

Socrates, so named because his father was interested in Greek mythology.
ITV commentator

Systems are made by players rather than players making systems.
Theo Foley

That shot might not have been as good as it might have been.
John Motson

That's a question mark everyone's asking.
Bruce Grobbelaar, goalkeeper and pundit

The acoustics seem to get louder.
Hugh Johns, ITV commentator

The goals made such a difference to the way this game went.
John Motson

The last player to score a hat-trick in a cup final was Stan Mortensen. He even had a final named after him, the Matthews final.
Lawrie McMenemy

The match has become quite unpredictable, but it still looks as though Arsenal will win the cup.
John Motson

The only thing I have in common with George Best is that we came from the same place, play for the same club and were discovered by the same man.
Norman Whiteside, Manchester United and Northern Ireland player

The only thing Norwich didn't get was the goal that they finally got.

Jimmy Greaves

There was a paradox of air in the town when we arrived in Watford this afternoon.

Andy Smith, player

They can crumble as easily as ice cream in this heat.

Sammy Nelson, Arsenal and Northern Ireland defender

This is a tremendous asset for the club, a tremendous head-ache lifted from our shoulders, really.

Elton John, Watford honorary life president

To me personally, it's nothing personal to me.

Ron Greenwood

Wallace, moving forward, his red hair always in the action.

Peter Jones

We are really quite lucky this year because Christmas falls on Christmas Day.

Bobby Gould, player and manager

We are really the victims of our own problems.

Jimmy Greaves

We could be putting the hammer in Luton's coffin.

Ray Wilkins, player, manager and pundit

Well, as for Ian Rush, he's perfectly fit, apart, that is, from his physical fitness.
    Mike England, Welsh BBC commentator

Well, Ibrox is filling up slowly, but rapidly.
    James Sanderson

Well, we got nine and you can't score more than that.
    Sir Bobby Robson

Whelan was in the position he was, exactly.
    Jimmy Armfield, player, manager and BBC Radio pundit

This is an unusual Scotland side because they have good players.
    Javier Clemente, Spanish football manager

I was surprised but, like I say, nothing surprises me in football.
    Les Ferdinand, England international

We didn't underestimate them. They were just a lot better than we thought.
    Sir Bobby Robson

If you're 0–0 down, there's no better person to get you back on terms than Ian Wright.
    Robbie Earle, player and pundit

I'd give my right arm to get back in the England team.
    Peter Shilton

Moving from Wales to Italy is like going to a different country.
    Ian Rush, Welsh international

If we played like this every week we wouldn't be so inconsistent.
  Sir Bobby Robson

The first ninety minutes of a football match are the most important.
  Sir Bobby Robson

Nice to see your home fans booing you – that's loyal supporters.
  Wayne Rooney after England's World Cup draw with
  Algeria in Cape Town

You've got to believe you're going to win, and I believe we will win the World Cup until the final whistle blows and we're knocked out.
  Peter Shilton

It's obviously a great occasion for all the players. It's a moment they will always forget.
  Ray Hudson

If you want to win the title, one thing you need is consistent consistency.
  Arsène Wenger

I can see the carrot at the end of the tunnel.
  Stuart Pearce, player and pundit

The manager still has a fresh pair of legs up his sleeve.
  John Greig, Scottish player, manager and pundit

Steve McCahill has limped off with a badly cut forehead.
  Tom Ferrie

The lads ran their socks into the ground.
  Sir Alex Ferguson

Suffice it to say that this will be remembered as a season best forgotten.
  Terry Baddoo, presenter

I've got a gut feeling in my stomach.
  Sir Alan Sugar, entrepreneur and football club owner

See also: REFEREES AND UMPIRES

GAMBLING

The urge to gamble is so universal and its practice so pleasurable that I assume it must be evil.
Heywood Broun, wit

There are two times in a man's life when he should not speculate: when he can't afford it, and when he can.
Mark Twain, American author

No dog can go as fast as the money you bet on him.
Bud Flanagan, comedian

I backed this horse at twenty to one – and it came in at twenty-five past four.
Anon.

Horse sense is the thing a horse has that keeps it from betting on people.
W. C. Fields, actor and comedian

A man's got to make at least one bet every day, otherwise he could be walking around lucky and never know it.
Jimmy Jones, wit

I figure you have the same chance of winning the lottery whether you play or not.

  Fran Lebowitz, author

Any man who has to save up to go racing has no right to be on a racecourse.

  Jeffrey Bernard, journalist

An ante-post bet is simply a way of prolonging life. A man holding an ante-post voucher never dies before the race.

  Jeffrey Bernard

I had a good day at the races. I didn't go.

  Anon.

The only man who makes money following the horses is one who does it with a broom and shovel.

  Elbert Hubbard, wit

Fellows become bookmakers because they are too scared to steal and too heavy to become a jockey.

  Noel Whitcome, journalist

The reason Con loses at the races, while he always wins at cards, is that he can't shuffle the horses!

  The Jockey Who Laughs

No one has ever bet enough on a winning horse.

  Richard Sasuly, writer, on gambling

I went to the racetrack today but it was shut, so I just pushed all my money through the gate.

  W. C. Fields

The way his horses ran could be summed up in a word – last.

Anon.

Many horses are given peculiar names – especially if they don't finish in the first three.

Anon.

My horse was so slow, he won the next race.

Anon.

I wouldn't bet on a horse unless he came up to my house and told me to himself.

Eubie Blake, ragtime pianist and composer

In most betting shops you will see three windows marked 'Bet Here', but only one window with the legend 'Pay Out'.

Jeffrey Bernard

The horse I bet on came in so late, that it had to tiptoe into the barn so's not to wake the other horses.

Anon.

A bookie is just a pickpocket who lets you use your own hands.

Henry Morgan, comedian

He once had a horse that finished ahead of the winner of the 1942 Kentucky Derby.

Unfortunately, the horse started running in the *1941* Kentucky Derby.

Groucho Marx, *Esquire*, 1972

My brother loves sick animals. Mind you, he doesn't know they're sick when he backs them.
  Sally Poplin, humorous writer

My horse came in so late, the jockey was wearing pyjamas.
  Anon.

Gambling: the sure way of getting nothing for something.
  Wilson Mizner, wit

See also: HORSES AND HORSE RACING

GOLF

Don Quixote would understand golf. It is the impossible dream.
Jim Murray, sportswriter

Although golf was originally restricted to wealthy, overweight Protestants, today it's open to anybody who owns hideous clothing.
Dave Barry, *Miami Herald*

The great thing about golf – and this is the reason why a lot of health experts like me recommend it – is you can drink beer and ride in a cart while you play.
Dave Barry

His doctor told him to play thirty-six holes a day, so he went out and bought a harmonica.
Anon.

Playing golf with the President is handy. If you hit a ball into the rough and it drops near a tree, the tree becomes a Secret Service man and moves away.
Bob Hope, comedian

One way to solve the problem of golfers' slow play is to knock the ball into them. There will be a short delay while you have a hell of a fight but from then on they'll move faster.

Horace Hutchinson, Victorian writer and 'the father of golf instruction'

The secret of missing a tree is to aim straight at it.

Michael Green, *The Art of Coarse Golf,* 1968

I was swinging like a toilet door on a prawn trawler.

David Feherty, golfer, writer, broadcaster

For me, the worst part of playing golf, by far, has always been hitting the ball.

Dave Barry, *Miami Herald*

Reggie's was a troubled spirit these days. He was in love, and he developed a bad slice with his mid-iron. He was practically a soul in torment.

P. G. Wodehouse, novelist

My backswing off the first tee put the pro in mind of an elderly woman of dubious morals trying to struggle out of a dress too tight around the shoulders.

Patrick Campbell, journalist and humorist

What does it profit a man if he gains the whole world and three-putts the eighteenth green?

Fred Corcoran, golfer and sports promoter

Watching Sam Snead practise hitting a golf ball is like watching a fish practise swimming.

John Schlee, American golfer

Good news: ten golfers a year are hit by lightning.

  George Carlin, comedian

I get upset over a bad shot just like anybody else, but it's silly to let the game get to you. When I miss a shot I just think what a beautiful day it is and what fresh pure air I'm breathing. Then I take a deep breath. I have to do that. That's what gives me the strength to break the club.

  Bob Hope

Jack Lemmon has been in more bunkers than Eva Braun.

  Phil Harris, singer, songwriter, comedian

Hubert Green swings like a drunk trying to find a keyhole in the dark.

  Jim Murray, of American golfer

I've just had a hole-in-one at the sixteenth and I left the ball in the hole just to prove it.

  Bob Hope

I can't cheat on my score – all you have to do is look back down the fairway and count the wounded.

  Bob Hope

In the rough at Muirfield not only could you lose your golf ball but if you left your golf bag down, you could lose that too. You could even lose a short caddy.

  Jack Nicklaus

Time was, if you had forty white men with sticks chasing a black man, it was the Ku Klux Klan. Nowadays it's the US Open.

  Martin Blake, Australian sportswriter

David Leadbetter wanted me to change my takeaway, my backswing, my downswing and my follow-through. He said I could still play right-handed.

Brad Bryant, Texan golfer of instructor

Is my friend in the bunker or is the bastard on the green?

David Feherty

The fairway is a narrow strip of mown grass that separates two groups of golfers looking for lost balls in the rough.

Henry Beard, humorist

A golfer needs a loving wife to whom he can describe the day's play through the long evening.

P. G. Wodehouse

The real test of golf – like life – is not keeping out of the rough, but getting out after we are in.

Henry Lash, golfer

I love golf. I live golf. I dream golf. If only I could *play* golf!

Anon.

When you're putting well, you are a good putter; when your opponent is putting well, he has a good putter.

John D. Sheridan, writer and humorist

I don't want to be a millionaire, I only want to live like one.

Walter Hagen, legendary American golfer

He's got a swing like an octopus putting up a deckchair.

Anon.

More lampshades were broken in Britain by golf clubs than by Hitler's bombers.

Val Doonican, entertainer

A coarse golfer is one who normally goes from tee to green without touching the fairway.

Michael Green, *The Art of Coarse Golf*, 1968

When male golfers wiggle their feet to get their stance right, they look exactly like cats preparing to pee.

Jilly Cooper, novelist

You can take a man's wife, you can even take his wallet, but never on any account take a man's putter.

Archie Compston, English golfer

Putts should be conceded only in the following circumstances:
1. When your opponent is two inches from the pin and three down.
2. Your opponent is 9 feet from the hole and is your boss.
3. Immediately after you have holed out in one.

Tom Scott, English golfer

There was never much said on the course when I played with Nick. I probably knew him twenty years before I heard him complete a sentence.

Paul Azinger, American golfer and analyst, of British golfer Nick Faldo

I owe everything to golf. Where else would a guy with an IQ like mine earn so much money?

Hubert Green, American golfer

I love playing golf. My only problem is that I stand too close to the ball after I've hit it.

Anon.

Tom Lehman's mannerisms are reminiscent of a highly competitive turtle.

Anon., of American golfer

It is now known that Darwin was a golfer. He set out in search of the missing links.

Sam Gross, American gag cartoonist

Paris is a beautiful city. I went to the Eiffel Tower, to the Louvre, something like that, and the archway, and saw the castle that we are staying next to [the Palace of Versailles].

Bubba Watson, American golfer

A professional will tell you the amount of flex you need in the shaft of your club. The more the flex, the more strength you will need to break the thing over your knees.

Stephen Baker, *How to Play Golf in the Low 120s*

The earthquake caused giant holes in the ground – but Monty still needed three putts to get down.

Derek McGovern, in the *Daily Mirror*

There are so many doglegs here, Lassie must have designed the course.

Bob Rosburg, TV analyst, of the Hazeltine National Golf Club, Minnesota

A hole-in-one is an occurrence in which a ball is hit directly from the tee into the hole on a single shot by a golfer playing alone.

Henry Beard and Roy McKie, *Golfing: A Duffer's Dictionary*

Having said that, no one remembers who finished second. But they still ask me if I ever think about that putt I missed to win the 1970 Open at St Andrews. I tell them that sometimes it doesn't cross my mind for a full five minutes.

Doug Sanders, American golfer

You ever watch golf on television? It's like watching flies f***.

George Carlin

When you get to my age, you don't buy green bananas.

Tom Watson, veteran golfer, discussing when he might retire

You lick the lollipop of mediocrity once and you'll suck forever.

Rory Sabbatini, South African golfer, Honda Classic winner

Let me put it to you this way: golf is really, really boring.

Jason Dufner, American golfer, 2012

The Ryder Cup team of Americans was comprised of eleven nice guys and Paul Azinger.

Seve Ballesteros, 1991

Drink ten beers and eat a tub of ice cream before you go to bed.

Carl Pettersson, Swedish golfer, reveals his training regime

I thought he acted like the south end of a northbound mule.
    Paul Azinger, of Tiger Woods, 2012

Golf got its name because all the other four-letter words were taken.
    Anon.

On beginning play, as many balls as may be required to obtain a satisfactory result may be played from the first tee... Everyone recognizes a good player needs to 'loosen up' but does not have time for the practice tee.
    Donald A. Metz

If a putt passes over the hole without dropping, it is deemed to have dropped. The law of gravity holds that any object attempting to maintain a position in the atmosphere without something to support it must drop. The law of gravity supersedes the law of golf.
    Donald A. Metz

A putt that stops close enough to the cup to inspire such comments as 'you could blow it in' may be blown in. This rule does not apply if the ball is more than three inches from the hole, because no one wants to make a travesty of the game.
    Donald A. Metz

A [golf] ball hitting a tree shall be deemed not to have hit the tree. Hitting a tree is simply bad luck and has no place in a scientific game. The player should estimate the distance the ball would have traveled if it had not hit the tree and play the ball from there, preferably atop a nice firm tuft of grass.
    Donald A. Metz

A (golf) ball sliced or hooked into the rough shall be lifted and placed in the fairway at a point equal to the distance it carried or rolled into the rough. Such veering right or left frequently results from friction between the face of the club and the cover of the ball and the player should not be penalized for the erratic behaviour of the ball resulting from such uncontrollable physical phenomena.

　　Donald A. Metz, *Rules of Golf for Good Players*

Members are requested not to pick up lost balls until they have stopped running.

　　Notice in golf club

Give me my golf clubs, the fresh air and a beautiful woman as a partner – and you can have the golf clubs and the fresh air.

　　George Burns, comedian

My golf is definitely improving. I'm missing the ball much closer than I used to.

　　Anon.

Last week I missed a spectacular hole in one – by only five strokes.

　　Anon.

My game is so bad I gotta hire three caddies – one to walk the left rough, one for the right rough, and one down the middle. And the one in the middle doesn't have to do much.

　　Dave Hill, American golfer

Real golfers, no matter what the provocation, never strike a caddie with the driver. The sand wedge is far more effective.

　　Huxtable Pippey, golfing wit

While tearing off
A game of golf
I may make a play for the caddy
But when I do
I don't follow through
'Cause my heart belongs to Daddy.
    Cole Porter, songwriter

If there's a faster way to turn a Jekyll into a Hyde than by handing a man the driver, we don't know of it.
    Lew Rushman, golfing wit

Man! I can't even point that far!
    Gay Brewer, golfer, on John Daly's driving power

When John Daly hits an iron he takes a cubic yard of Kent as well. His divots go further than my drives.
    David Feherty

My golfing partner couldn't hit a tiled floor with a bellyful of puke.
    David Feherty

Colin Montgomerie has a face like a warthog that has been stung by a wasp.
    David Feherty

Colin Montgomerie is a few fries short of a Happy Meal. His mind goes on vacation and leaves his mouth in charge.
    David Feherty

Colin Montgomerie couldn't count his balls and get the same answer twice.
    David Feherty

Jim Furyk has a swing like a man trying to kill a snake in a phone booth.

David Feherty

John Daly has the worst haircut I've ever seen in my life. It looks like he has a divot over each ear.

David Feherty

I don't know him but I've seen him smile, and that's quite enough to put me off wanting to know anything about him.

David Feherty, of Phil Mickelson

The only time Nick Faldo opens his mouth is to change feet.

David Feherty, on the British golfer

You look at Faldo and you have to resist the temptation to look at the back for the knobs.

Jim Murray, *Los Angeles Times*, of English golfer Nick Faldo

Corey Pavin plays the game as if he has a plane to catch; as if he were double-parked and left the meter running. Guys move slower leaving hotel fires.

Jim Murray

The man who once ruled it as smoothly as Bob Charles is presently putting more like Ray Charles.

Mark Reason of José María Olazábal

Golf balls are attracted to water as unerringly as the eye of a middle-aged man to a female bosom.

Michael Green, humorous writer

If you are going to throw a club, it is important to throw it ahead of you, down the fairway, so you don't waste energy going back to pick it up.

Tommy Bolt, American golfer

Never bet with anyone you meet on the first tee who has a deep suntan, a one-iron in his bag and squinty eyes.

Dave Marr, golfer and sportscaster

Never try to keep more than 300 separate thoughts in your mind during your swing.

Henry Beard

There are over 150 golf courses in the Palm Springs area and Gerry Ford is never sure which one he's going to play until his second shot.

Bob Hope, of the former President

Bob Hope has a beautiful short game. Unfortunately, it's off the tee.

Jimmy Demaret, American golfer

The definition of the average golfer is: one who starts at six, shouts 'Fore!', takes five, and puts down a three.

Anon.

The hardest shot is the chip at ninety yards from the green where the ball has to be played against an oak tree, bounces back into a sandtrap, hits a stone, bounces onto the green, and then rolls into the cup. That shot is so difficult, I have only made it once.

Zeppo Marx, comedian

Golf is a game of expletives not deleted.
  Irving Gladstone, golf writer

Show me a man who is a good loser and I'll show you a man who is playing golf with his boss.
  Sally Poplin, English humorous writer

Golf is a game to be played between cricket and death.
  Colin Ingleby-Mackenzie, England cricketer

I refuse to play golf with Errol Flynn. If you want to play with that prick, I'll play with my own.
  W. C. Fields, actor

He's hopeless. He's the only golfer I know who shouts 'Fore!' when he putts.
  Anon.

If you want to take long walks, take long walks. If you want to hit things with a stick, hit things with a stick. But there's no excuse for combining the two and putting the results on TV. Golf is not so much a sport as an insult to lawns.
  National Lampoon, 1979

Oh the dirty little pill
Went rolling down the hill
And rolled right into the bunker
From there to the green
I took thirteen
And then by God I sunk her!
  Traditional

The difference between learning to play golf and learning to drive a car is that in golf you never hit anything.

Anon.

Your financial cost of playing golf can best be figured out when you realise if you were to devote the same time and energy to business instead of golf, you would be a millionaire in approximately six weeks.

Buddy Hackett, actor and comedian

'After all, golf is only a game,' said Millicent.

Women say these things without thinking. It does not mean that there is any kink in their character. They simply don't realise what they are saying.

P. G. Wodehouse, *The Clicking of Cuthbert*, 1922

'Mortimer, you must choose between golf and me.'

'But, darling, I went round in a hundred and one yesterday. You can't expect a fellow to give up golf when he is at the top of his game.'

P. G. Wodehouse

The least thing upsets him on the links. He misses short putts because of the uproar of the butterflies in the adjoining meadows.

P. G. Wodehouse

Golf is a game whose aim is to hit a very small ball into an even smaller hole, with weapons singularly ill-designed for the purpose.

Winston Churchill

If I had my way, any man guilty of golf would be ineligible for any office of trust in the United States.
    H. L. Mencken, wit

Last year Jim took up golf with his usual boyish enthusiasm. He tells me he's delighted with his progress – just last Sunday, for instance, he managed to hit the ball in one.
    Anon.

You can always tell the golfer who's winning. He's the one who keeps telling his opponent that it's only a game.
    Sally Poplin

Golf is a good walk spoiled.
    Mark Twain

Golf is a game in which a ball [one and a half inches in diameter] is placed on a ball [eight thousand miles in diameter].
    The object being to hit the small ball but not the larger.
    John Cunningham, writer

I know I'm getting better at golf because I'm hitting fewer spectators.
    Gerald Ford, American President

The only times my prayers are never answered is when I'm on the golf course.
    Billy Graham, American preacher

There were three things in the world that he held in the smallest esteem: slugs, poets and caddies with hiccups.

P. G. Wodehouse, *The Heart of a Goof*, 1926

Golf is the infallible test... The man who can go into a patch of rough alone, with the knowledge that only God is watching him, and play his ball where it lies is the man who will serve you faithfully and well.

P. G. Wodehouse

Statisticians estimate that crime among good golfers is lower than in any class of the community except possibly bishops.

P. G. Wodehouse

Love has had a lot of press-agenting from the oldest times, but there are higher, nobler things than love. A woman is only a woman, but a hefty drive is still a slosh.

P. G. Wodehouse

Like all Saturday foursomes it is in difficulties. One of the patients is zigzagging about the fairway like a liner pursued by submarines.

P. G. Wodehouse

He enjoys that perfect peace, that peace beyond all understanding, which comes at its maximum only to the man who has given up golf.

P. G. Wodehouse

The uglier a man's legs are, the better he plays golf. It's almost a law.

H. G. Wells, *Bealby*, 1915

At least I hit two good balls today. I stepped on a rake.
Anon.

A golf course is nothing but a poolroom moved outdoors.
Barry Fitzgerald, actor

Sunday is the day all of us bow our heads. Some are praying and some are putting.
Anon.

The secret of good golf is to hit the ball hard, straight and not too often.
Anon.

Golf combines two favorite American pastimes: taking long walks and hitting things with a stick.
P. J. O'Rourke, writer

Golf is a day spent in a round of strenuous idleness.
William Wordsworth, poet

Golf is like chasing a quinine pill around a cow pasture.
Winston Churchill

Golf is so popular simply because it is the best game in the world at which to be bad.
A. A. Milne, novelist

I can airmail the golf ball, but sometimes I don't put the right address on it.
Jim Dent, golfer

I regard golf as an expensive way of playing marbles.
G. K. Chesterton, novelist

If a lot of people gripped a knife and fork the way they do a golf club, they'd starve to death.

Sam Snead, golfer

If there is any larceny in a man, golf will bring it out.

Paul Gallico, novelist

If you drink, don't drive. Don't even putt.

Dean Martin, singer

The reason the pro tells you to keep your head down is so you can't see him laughing.

Phyllis Diller, comedienne

These greens are so fast I have to hold my putter over the ball and hit it with the shadow.

Sam Snead

When I die, bury me on the golf course so my husband will visit.

Anon.

The number of shots taken by an opponent who is out of sight is equal to the square root of the sum of the number of curses heard plus the number of swishes.

Michael Green

The nice things about these golf books is that they usually cancel each other out. One book tells you to keep your eye on the ball; the next says not to bother. Personally, in the crowd I play with, a better idea is to keep your eye on your partner.

Jim Murray, *Los Angeles Times*

Only the other day I actually saw someone laugh on a posh golf course in Surrey.
    Michael Green

The rest of the field.
    Roger Maltbie, golfer, on being asked, before his final
    round, what he had to shoot to win the tournament.

Don't play too much golf. Two rounds a day are plenty.
    Harry Vardon, English golfer

His driving is unbelievable. I don't go that far on my holidays.
    Ian Baker-Finch, Australian golfer, on John Daly

I don't like watching golf on TV. I can't stand whispering.
    David Brenner, comedian

Carnoustie is like an ugly, old hag who speaks the truth no matter how painful. But it's only when you add up your score you hear exactly what she thinks of you.
    Tom Watson, on historic championship golf course in
    Angus, Scotland

Pebble Beach is so exclusive even the Samaritans have an unlisted number.
    Peter Dobereiner, commentator, on Californian golf course

Muirfield without a wind is like a lady undressed. No challenge.
    Tom Watson, on the Scottish golf course

I play in the low 80s. If it's any hotter than that, I won't play.
  Joe E. Lewis, comedian and actor

When I tee the ball where I can see it, I can't hit it.
And when I put it where I can hit it, I can't see it.
  Jackie Gleason, comedian, on his portly frame

The safest place for spectators in celebrity tournaments is
probably on the fairway.
  Joe Garagiola

A distinguished professor of pathology, who recently holed
out in one at the fourth at Walton Heath, thus opening the
round 4, 3, 7, 1, 4, 4, 4, asks whether he is the only man
in history to have started a round of golf with his own
telephone number.
  Henry Longhurst, writer and commentator

Gay Brewer swings the club in a figure of eight. If you didn't
know better, you'd swear he was trying to kill snakes.
  Dave Hill, famously outspoken golfer

Golf is not a sport. Golf is men in ugly pants, walking.
  Rosie O'Donnell, comedienne

The most exquisitely satisfying act in the world of golf is
that of throwing a club. The full backswing, the delayed
wrist action, the flowing follow-through, followed by that
unique whirring sound, reminiscent only of a passing flock
of starlings, are without parallel in sport.
  Henry Longhurst

A golfer is a guy who can walk eight miles with a heavy bag of clubs, but when he gets home expects his dog to fetch his slippers.

Anon.

A golf cart is a two-wheeled bag-carrier that decreases the exercise value of playing 18 holes of golf from about the level of two sets of doubles tennis to the equivalent of an hour and a half of shopping.

Henry Beard

The difference between a good golf shot and a bad one is the same as the difference between a beautiful woman and a plain one – a matter of millimetres.

Ian Fleming, *Goldfinger*, 1959

Those golfers who look as though they got dressed in the dark should be penalised two strokes each for offending the public eye.

Doug Sanders, American golfer

'Play It As It Lies' is one of the fundamental dictates of golf. The other one is 'Wear It If It Clashes'.

Henry Beard

It looks like a direct hit on a pizza factory.

Dave Marr, on David Duval's multi-coloured shirt

Few pleasures on earth match the feeling that comes from making a loud bodily-function noise just as a guy is about to putt.

Dave Barry, *Miami Herald*

Why am I using a new putter? Because the old one didn't float too well.

Craig Stadler, American golfer

It's a great golf hole. It gives you a million options, not one of them worth a damn.

Tom Kite, American golfer, of the 13th at St Andrews, the hole O' Cross (In)

The greatest thing to come out of Spain since a painting by Picasso that made sense.

Dan Jenkins, author and sportswriter, of Seve Ballesteros

The only place Seve Ballesteros turns up for nothing is at his mum's for breakfast.

Howard Clark, English golfer

And the wind shall say: 'Here were decent godless people; Their only monument the asphalt road. And a thousand lost golf balls.'

T. S. Eliot, 'Choruses of the Rock'

Golfers don't fist fight. They cuss a bit. But they wouldn't punch anything or anybody. They might hurt their hands and have to change their grip.

Dan Jenkins, *Dead Solid Perfect*, 1988

They say that President Taft,
When hit by a golf ball, once laughed
And said, 'I'm not sore,
Although he called Fore,
The place where he hit me was aft!'

Anon.

Art Rosenbaum said he wanted to get more distance. I told him to hit it and run backwards.

Ken Venturi, golfer and broadcaster, of the *San Francisco Chronicle* writer

David Duval has gone from best player never to have won a major to worst player who has.

Michael Ventre, TV writer

However unlucky you may be on the golf course, it really is not fair to expect your adversary's grief for your undeserved misfortunes to be as poignant as your own.

Horace Hutchinson

If your adversary is badly bunkered, there is no rule against your standing over him and counting his strokes aloud, with increasing gusto as their number mounts up; but it will be a wise precaution to arm yourself with the niblick before doing so, so as to meet him on equal terms.

Horace Hutchinson

Should you cut up turf, be careful to replace it, golf is not agriculture.

Horace Hutchinson

If you think it's hard to meet new people, try picking up the wrong golf ball.

Jack Lemmon, American actor

May thy ball lie in green pastures ... and not in still waters.

Anon.

You can hit a 200-acre fairway 10 per cent of the time and a 2-inch branch 90 per cent of the time.
  Henry Beard

He took a swing like a man with a wasp under his shirt and his pants on fire, trying to impale a butterfly on the end of a scythe.
  Paul Gallico, novelist and sportswriter

The most common mistake at St Andrews is just turning up.
  Mark James, English golfer

The difference between a sand bunker and water is the difference between a car crash and an airplane crash. You have a chance of recovering from a car crash.
  Bobby Jones, American golfer

It hit a spectator, but my ball is OK.
  Jerry Pate, American golfer

It's a marriage. If I had to choose between my wife and my putter, I'd miss her.
  Gary Player

I'm pretty calm and cool out there. He might be borderline dead, but I think it's a good thing.
  Zach Johnson, on his Ryder Cup partner Jason Dufner's on-course demeanour, 2012

I've hit two balls into the water. I've a good mind to jump in and make it four.
  Simon Hobday, South African golfer

We hear guys talking about needing swing coaches, sports psychologists, fitness instructors or changing managers. He needs an exorcist. I half expect winged bulls to fly out of his head when he is standing over a shot.

Brandel Chamblee, on Kevin Na's pre-shot problems, 2012

INDIVIDUAL GOLFERS

Walter Hagen

No one remembers who came second.

You're only here for a short visit. Don't hurry, don't worry. And be sure to smell the flowers along the way.

Bobby Jones

The secret of golf is to turn three shots into two.

It's nothing new or original to say that golf is played one stroke at a time. But it took me many years to realise it.

Competitive golf is played on a five and a half inch course – the space between your ears.

Jack Nicklaus

Tee the ball high. Because years of experience have shown me that air offers less resistance to dirt.

It's hard not to play golf that is up to Jack Nicklaus's standard when you are Jack Nicklaus.

Golf is a better game played downhill.

I think I fail a bit less than everyone else.
  When asked about the secret of his success.

I finally discovered the secret of the Old Course at St Andrews. Take fewer putts.

I was thinking I might go out and play like Jack Nicklaus, but instead it's more like Jacques Tati.
  David Feherty

If Jack Nicklaus had to play my tee shots, he couldn't break 80. He'd be a pharmacist with a string of drugstores in Ohio.
  Lee Trevino

Arnold Palmer

What other people find in poetry or art museums, I find in the flight of a good drive.

I once got a ball out of a St Andrews bunker in two. I'm not saying God couldn't have got it out in one, but He would have had to throw it.

Sam Snead's got more money buried underground than I ever made on top. He's got gophers in his backyard that subscribe to *Fortune*. He's packed more coffee cans than Brazil.

How did I make a twelve on a par-five hole? It's simple – I missed a 4-foot putt for an eleven.

I have a tip that can take five strokes off anyone's golf game: it's called an eraser.

Being paired with Arnold Palmer is like a two-shot penalty.
John Schlee, fellow pro

He went out to mug the course. He went out to give the course a beating.
Ernie Els, South African golfer

Arnold Palmer had everything except a brake pedal.
Peter Dobereiner, *Golf Digest*

Arnold Palmer is the biggest crowd-pleaser since the invention of the portable sanitary facility.
Bob Hope

Palmer hitched up his baggy pants and turned golf into a game of 'Hit it hard, go find it and hit it hard again.'
John Schulian, sportswriter

Arnie would go for the flag from the middle of an alligator's back.
Lee Trevino

Palmer lashes into the ball with such explosive force that he almost falls off the tee after his follow through.
Billy Casper, golfer

Chi Chi Rodriguez

It's still embarrassing. I asked my caddie for a sand wedge and ten minutes later he came back with a ham on rye.

I never pray to God to make a putt. I pray to God to help me react good if I miss a putt.

I never exaggerate. I just remember big.

For most amateurs the best wood in the bag is the pencil.

The first time I played the Masters I was so nervous I drank a bottle of rum before I teed off. I shot the happiest 83 of my life.

If I'm going to putt and miss, I want to look good doing it.
   On refusing to use a long-handled putter

Lee Trevino

You don't know what pressure is in golf until you play for five bucks with only two in your pocket.

Columbus went round the world in 1492.
That isn't a lot of strokes when you consider the course.

I once 'skyed' a ball so high, I had to shout, 'Don't touch it Lord, there's a two-stroke penalty if you do.'

You can talk to a fade but a hook won't listen.

They say I'm famous for my chip shots. Sure, when I hit 'em right, they land just so, like a butterfly with sore feet.

There are two things not long for this world – dogs that chase cars and pro golfers who chip for pars.

No one who ever had lessons would have a swing like mine.

If it wasn't for golf, I don't know what I'd be doing. If my IQ had been two points lower, I'd have been a tree somewhere.

Why would I want to be out there with all those young guns? No sense playing the flat bellies when you can play the round bellies.

On becoming eligible for the Senior Tour

They say, 'Trevino is wondering whether to play a five or six iron to the green', when all the time I'm gazing at some broad in the third row of the gallery, wondering where my wife is.

My swing is so bad I look like a caveman killing his lunch.

At fifteen, we put down my bag to hunt for a ball; found the ball, lost the bag.

In the rough at Royal Birkdale, Lancashire

The first one is called *How to Get the Most Distance out of Your Shanks* and the other is *How to Take the Correct Stance on Your Fourth Putt*.

On his proposed book titles

I adore the game of golf. I won't ever retire. I'll play until I die. Then I want them to roll me into a bunker, cover me with sand and make sure nobody's ball lands in there for a while.

There are two things you can do with your head down – play golf and pray.

Golf architects can't play golf themselves, and they make damn sure that no one else can.

I plan to win so much money this year, my caddie's gonna finish in the Top 20 money winners.

You can make a lot of money out of golf. Ask any of my ex-wives.

I'm not saying my golf game went bad, but if I grew tomatoes they'd come up sliced.

I'm like a 1967 Cadillac. I've changed the engine twice, rolled back the odometer and replaced the transmission. But now all the tyres are going flat, it's time to put it in the junkyard.

I'm hitting the driver so good, I gotta dial the operator for long distance after I hit it.

If there is a thunderstorm on a golf course, walk down the middle of the fairway holding a one-iron over your head. Even God can't hit a one-iron.

If conversation was fertiliser, Lee Trevino would be up to his neck in grass all the time.

Larry Ziegler, American golfer

If Lee Trevino didn't have an Adam's apple, he'd have no shape at all.

Gary Player

Bob Hope – Comedian

I would like to deny all allegations by Bob Hope that during my last game of golf I hit an eagle, a birdie, an elk and a moose.

Gerald Ford

I've done as much for golf as Truman Capote has for sumo wrestling.

Jack Benny had only one golf ball the whole of his golfing career. He finally lost it when the string came off.

Sammy Davis Jr hits the ball 130 yards and his jewellery goes 150.

Some of these legends have been around golf a long time. When they mention a good grip, they're talking about their dentures.

When I play with Gerald Ford, I usually try to make it a four-some – the President, myself, a paramedic and a faith healer.

I'll shoot my age if I have to live to be 105.

GAFFES AND BLOOPERS

The par here at Sunningdale is 70 and anything under that will mean a score in the 60s.
  Steve Rider, commentator, on English golf course

And now to hole 8 which is in fact the eighth hole.
  Peter Alliss, golfer and commentator

He certainly didn't appear as cool as he looked.
  Renton Laidlaw, commentator

He used to be fairly indecisive, but now he's not so certain.
  Peter Alliss, golfer and commentator

I owe a lot to my parents, especially to mother and my father.
  Greg Norman, golfer

Piñero has missed the putt, I wonder what he's thinking in Spanish.
  Renton Laidlaw

There he stands with his legs akimbo.
  Peter Alliss

GYMNASTICS

My question about women's gymnastics is simple. Are we not supposed to be looking at their little rear ends while they're jumping around all over the place? Because I think that's pretty much all I've been doing, and I don't know if it's wrong. I mean, if it's wrong, I'll stop, but no one's ever said anything about it. The announcer never goes, 'In judging this event they throw out the high score, the low score, and stop staring at their little rear ends.'

Jerry Seinfeld, *SeinLanguage*, 1993

HORSES AND HORSE RACING

Jockey (Flat):
An anorexic dwarf in bright colours who drives a large car with cushions on the seat and blocks on the pedals.

Jockey (Jump):
Punch-drunk, nobbly, occasionally hot-headed individual who must be as stupid as he looks to take 100 times as many risks as the flat counterpart for one hundredth of the rewards.
    Anon.

I once backed a horse which finished in front of the winner in the 1999 Grand National. Unfortunately, the horse started running in the 1998 Grand National.
    Anon.

It takes a good deal of physical courage to ride a horse. This, however, I have. I get it at about forty cents a flask, and take it as required.
    Stephen Leacock, political scientist and humorist

There are no handles to a horse but the 1910 model has a string to each side of its face for turning its head when there is anything you want it to see.

Stephen Leacock

To own a racehorse is the equivalent of burning a yacht on the front lawn every year.

Adam Nicholson, author and historian

Bill Shoemaker didn't ride a horse, he joined them. Most riders beat horses as if they were guards in slave-labour camps. Shoe treated them as if he were asking them to dance.

Jim Murray, *Los Angeles Times*

If you could call the thing a horse. If it hadn't shown a flash of speed in the straight, it would have got mixed up with the next race.

P. G. Wodehouse, *Very Good, Jeeves*, 1930

I just played a horse yesterday so slow the jockey kept a diary of the trip.

Henny Youngman, 1940

If you hit a pony over the nose at the outset of your acquaintance, he may not love you but he will take a deep interest in your movements ever afterwards.

Rudyard Kipling, poet and novelist

I am a jockey because I was too small to be a window cleaner and too big to be a garden gnome.

Adrian Maguire, Irish jockey and trainer

Edmund: You ride a horse rather less well than another horse would.

> Richard Curtis and Rowan Atkinson, *The Black Adder*,
> 'The Black Seal', BBC TV, 1983

Tell them you've got the flu.

> Lester Piggott, champion jockey, responding to trainer
> Jeremy Tree's plea: 'I've got to speak to my old school,
> Lester, and tell them all I know about racing. What should
> I tell them?'

There are fools, damn fools, and jockeys who remount in a steeplechase.

> John Oaksey, jockey, journalist and commentator

One way to stop a runaway horse is to bet on him.

> Jeffrey Bernard, wit

People ask me why I ride with my bottom in the air. Well, I've got to put it somewhere.

> Lester Piggott

A tremendous race, with four finishers out of thirty starters, so that by the end there were far more BBC commentators than horses.

> Clive James, TV critic, on the 1980 Grand National

Secretariat is everything I am not. He is young, he has lots of hair, he is fast, he has a large bank account and his entire sex life is before him.

> Cy Burick, *Dayton Daily News*, of a thoroughbred racehorse

Secretariat and Riva Ridge are the most famous pair of stablemates since Joseph and Mary.
  Dick Schaap, racing writer

It was the plainest Oaks field I have ever seen, and the paddock critic who expressed a decided preference for the horse of the policewoman on duty was no bad judge.
  Roger Mortimer, *Sunday Times*

If a horse is no good, trade him for a dog, then shoot the dog.
  Ben Jones, trainer

If I never hear another interview with the terminally irritating Frankie Dettori, I will not feel my life to be significantly impoverished.
  Martin Kelner, much-missed *Guardian* columnist and
  broadcaster

When interviewing Lester Piggott, an answer as third as long as the question is the standard rate of exchange.
  Hugh McIlvanney, British sportswriter

He don't talk to me and I don't talk to him. Other than that, we get along real fine.
  Sonny Hine, American trainer, of fellow trainer Bob Baffert

You could remove the brains from 90 per cent of jockeys and they would still weigh the same.
  John Francome, English jockey

A loose horse is any horse sensible enough to get rid of its rider at an early stage and carry on unencumbered.
    Clive James

The stewards demand explanations
But listen with cynical looks.
It's obvious in their estimations
That trainers are all licensed crooks.
    Anon.

At one time a little humdrum adultery could prove a barrier to the Royal Enclosure at Ascot, but now something rather more spectacular is required, such as hijacking a Securicor van or taking too prominent a role in a sex-instruction film designed for circulation in the best preparatory schools.
    Roger Mortimer, *Sunday Times*

The simple truth is that some of our racecourses are so poorly run and unimaginatively managed, and couldn't attract extra customers if Arkle, Desert Orchid, Nijinsky and the Archangel Gabriel all appeared on the same card.
    Sporting Life

There are three racecourses beginning with the letter F – namely Fontwell, Folkestone and effing Plumpton.
    Fred Winter, jockey, attrib.

You might have imagined that Harvey Smith was mounted on a piece of stereo equipment, but Sanyo Music Centre, though it has a leg in each corner like certain types of radio-gram, is in fact a living creature with no provision for the electronic reproduction of sound.
    Clive James

A real racehorse should have a head like a lady and the behind like a cook.

Jack Leach, jockey and tipster

With some justification the Jockey Club has been described as 'the purest example of the eighteenth century to survive in Britain'.

John Purvis, wit

Horses and jockeys mature earlier than people – which is why horses are admitted to racetracks at the age of two, and jockeys before they are old enough to shave.

Dick Beddoes, *Toronto Globe and Mail* columnist

I know you, you're the jockey who got tired before his horse.

Man in street, to John Oaksey after he had surrendered his lead on Carrickbeg in the last 25 yards of the 1963 Grand National

I follow the horses. And the horses I follow, follow horses.

Joe E. Lewis, comedian and actor

There is little to compare with the thrill of standing next to the creature in the winner's enclosure avoiding his hooves and receiving the congratulations of the press, your trainer and friends who backed it. What makes the experience so satisfying is that you, the owner, have had absolutely nothing to do with the horse winning.

Robert Morley, actor and wit

You never see a pretty, unattached girl on a racecourse. But you often see positive gangs of rather un-pretty ones. They are the owners or the owners' wives and they wear mink in all weathers and far too much make-up. For some odd reason, I can never work out why they always seem to be married to haulage contractors in the North, builders in the South and farmers in the West.

    Jeffrey Bernard

I have stood in a bar in Lambourn and been offered, in the space of five minutes, a poached salmon, a leg of a horse, a free trip to Chantilly, marriage, a large unsolicited loan, ten tips for a ten-horse race, two second-hand cars, a fight, and the copyright to a dying jockey's life story.

    Jeffrey Bernard, of a town noted for its association with
    National Hunt racing

If Jesus Christ rode his flaming donkey like you just rode that horse, then he deserved to be crucified.

    Fred Rimell, National Hunt jockey and trainer, to amateur
    jockey Jim Old

You never have to run after the winner, asking him for a few words.

    Earl Wilson, columnist, on why horse racing is easier to
    cover for a sports journalist

If you want to understand the effect of weight on a horse, try running for a bus with nothing in your hands. Then try doing it with your hands full of shopping. Then think about doing that for four-and-a-half miles.

    Jenny Pitman, English trainer

There is nothing better for the inside of a man than the outside of a horse.

Ronald Reagan, former President of the United States

GAFFES AND BLOOPERS

He's a very competitive competitor, that's the sort of competitor he is.

Dorian Williams, British equestrian and show jumping commentator

There's Pam watching anxiously. She doesn't look anxious though.

Stephen Hadley, show jumping commentator

These two horses have met five times this season, and I think they've beaten each other on each occasion.

Jimmy Lindley, jockey and commentator

Willie Carson, riding his 180th winner of the season, spent the last two furlongs looking over one shoulder then another, even between his legs, but there was nothing there to worry him.

Sporting Life

A racing horse is not like a machine. It has to be tuned up like a racing car.

Chris Pool, commentator

Rodeo-ing is about the only sport you can't fix. You'd have to talk to the bulls and horses, and they wouldn't understand you.

Bill Linderman, rodeo cowboy, 1954

See also: GAMBLING

HUNTING AND SHOOTING

The English country gentleman galloping after a fox – the unspeakable in full pursuit of the uneatable.
  Oscar Wilde, *A Woman of No Importance*, 1893

A sportsman is a man who, every now and then, simply has to go out and kill something.
  Stephen Leacock, Canadian political scientist and humorist

A man out hunting in the Highlands today climbed over a fence with his rifle cocked. He is survived by his wife, three children and one rabbit.
  Anon.

I have hunted deer on occasions but they were not aware of it.
  Felix Gear, writer

Support the Right to Arm Bears!
  Anti-hunting slogan

I'm all for hunters having guns. Or anything else that increases the chances of two rednecks blowing each other's heads off.
  Bobcat Goldthwait, American comedian

My uncle is a great tracker. He once followed these tracks into a cave and shot a train.

Anon.

I always will remember,
'twas a year ago November,
I went out to hunt some deer
On a mornin' bright and clear.
I went and shot the maximum the game laws would allow,
Two game wardens, seven hunters, and a cow.

I was in no mood to trifle,
I took down my trusty rifle and went out to stalk my prey.
What a haul I made that day.
I tied them to my fender, and I drove them home somehow,
Two game wardens, seven hunters, and a cow.

The law was very firm, it
Took away my permit,
The worst punishment I ever endured.
It turned out there was a reason,
Cows were out of season,
And one of the hunters wasn't insured...

Tom Lehrer, 'The Hunting Song'

We'll be talking to a gunsmith who's invented a sage-and-onion bullet that shoots the goose and stuffs it at the same time.

The Two Ronnies, BBC TV

If God didn't want man to hunt, he wouldn't have given us plaid shirts.

Johnny Carson, *The Tonight Show*, NBC TV

The hunter came across a sign that read: BEAR LEFT. So he gave up and went home.

Anon.

I only kill in self-defense. What would you do if a rabbit pulled a knife on you?

Johnny Carson, *The Tonight Show*, NBC TV

Lady Utterwold: ... everybody can see that the people who hunt are the right people and the people who don't are the wrong ones.

George Bernard Shaw, *Heartbreak House*, 1919

No sportsman wants to kill the fox or the pheasant as I want to kill him when I see him doing it.

George Bernard Shaw

Ok, I said to myself as I sighted the bird down the end of the gun. This time, my fine feathered friend, there is no escape.

Boris Johnson, mayor of London, *Friends, Voters, Countrymen*, 2001

... makes me want to shout from St Paul's steeple,
The people I'd like to shoot are the shooting people.

Howard Dietz, *By Myself*, 1937

PARDON MY DRIVING – I'M RELOADING

Bumper sticker, Florida 2012

Q: Who always has the right of way?
A: The car with a gun rack and a bumper sticker that reads,
   GUNS DON'T KILL PEOPLE, I DO.
   Anon.

Grouse shooting begins on 12 August. A grouse shot before
that date tends to be very annoyed.
   Michael Shea, Scottish polymath

ICE HOCKEY

You miss 100 per cent of the shots you never take.
Wayne Gretzky, legendary hockey player

Ice hockey? Isn't that the game where you take a stick and hit the puck, or anyone who has recently hit the puck?
Anon.

An assault in hockey, or, as they call it in the hood, 'white-on-white crime'.
Jay Leno, late-night host

I'll fine any of my players who wins the Lady Byng Trophy for ice hockey gentlemanly conduct.
Punch Imlach, NHL coach and general manager

Hockey's the only place where a guy can go nowadays and watch two white guys fight.
Frank Deford, sportswriter

Hockey belongs to the Cartoon Network, where a person can be pancaked by an ACME anvil, then expanded – accordion-style – back to full stature, without any lasting side effect.
Steve Rushin, journalist and speaker

Red ice sells hockey tickets.
  Bob Stewart, Canadian defenceman

I like to skate on the other side of the ice.
  Steven Wright, stand-up

Some people skate to the puck. I skate to where the puck is going to be.
  Wayne Gretzky

If they don't put a stop to the fighting at ice hockey matches, we'll have to start printing more tickets.
  Conn Smythe, Canadian player and businessman

Ice hockey players can walk on water.
  Anon.

Hockey players have fire in their hearts and ice in their veins.
  Anon.

The name 'February' comes from the Latin word 'Februarius', which means 'fairly boring stretch of time during which one expects the professional ice-hockey season to come to an end but it does not'.
  Dave Barry, *Miami Herald*

Hockey is murder on ice.
  Jim Murray, *Los Angeles Times* sportswriter

Street hockey is great for kids. It's energetic, competitive, and skilful. And best of all it keeps them off the street.
  Anon.

Hockey captures the essence of Canadian experience in the New World. In a land so inescapably and inhospitably cold, hockey is the chance of life, and an affirmation that despite the deathly chill of winter we are alive.

Stephen Leacock, humorist

Goaltending is a normal job, sure. How would you like it in your job if every time you made a small mistake, a red light went on over your desk and 15,000 people stood up and yelled at you?

Jacques Plante, Canadian goaltender

If you've only got one day to live, come see the Toronto Maple Leafs. It'll seem like forever.

Pat Foley, play-by-play announcer for the Chicago Blackhawks

Ice hockey is a form of disorderly conduct in which the score is kept.

Doug Larson, columnist

By the age of eighteen, the average American has witnessed 200,000 acts of violence on television, most of them occurring during Game 1 of the NHL playoff series.

Steve Rushin, journalist and speaker

Canada is a country whose main exports are ice hockey players and cold fronts. Our two main imports are baseball players and acid rain.

Pierre Trudeau, former Prime Minister

October is not only a beautiful month but marks the precious yet fleeting overlap of hockey, baseball, basketball, and football.

Jason Love

Half the game is mental; the other half is being mental.
 Jim McKenny

A puck is a hard rubber disc that hockey players strike when they can't hit one another.
 Jimmy Cannon, sportswriter

Give blood. Play hockey.
 Anon.

I went to a fight the other night, and a hockey game broke out.
 Rodney Dangerfield, comedian

Hockey players wear numbers because you can't always identify the body with dental records.
 Anon.

Don't go through life without goals.
 Ice hockey proverb

Hockey is figure skating in a war zone.
 Anon.

High sticking, tripping, slashing, spearing, charging, hooking, fighting, unsportsmanlike conduct, interference, roughing ... everything else is just figure skating.
 Anon.

Baseball happens to be a game of cumulative tension but football, basketball and hockey are played with hand grenades and machine guns.
 John Leonard

Four out of five dentists surveyed recommended playing hockey.
 Anon.

All hockey players are bilingual. They know English and profanity.

Gordie Howe

My goal is to deny yours.

Hockey saying

When Hell freezes over, I'll play hockey there too.

Anon.

Black people dominate sports in the United States – 20 per cent of the population and 90 per cent of the Final Four. We own this s***. Basketball, baseball, football, golf, tennis and as soon as they make a heated hockey rink we'll take that s*** too.

Chris Rock, stand-up

We get nose jobs all the time in the NHL, and we don't even have to go to the hospital.

Brad Park, New York Rangers defenceman

See also: WINTER SPORTS

KARATE

My brother-in-law died. He was a karate expert, then joined the army. The first time he saluted, he killed himself.
  Henny Youngman, stand-up

My neighbourhood is so bad I started taking karate lessons. I learned how to break my hand in half by hitting a brick.
  David Corrado, writer and comedian

I don't like to brag or frighten, but I've got a black belt. And a brown one, which I sometimes wear with black slacks.
  Jarod Kintz, humorous writer

Karate is a form of martial arts in which people who have had years and years of training can, using only their hands and feet, make some of the worst movies in the history of the world.
  Dave Barry, *Miami Herald*

Q: What is the difference between judo and karate?
A: Karate is an ancient form of self defence, and judo is what they make bagels out of.
  Anon.

See also BOXING, WRESTLING

LACROSSE

Lacrosse: Chix with Stix
   T-shirt slogan

They thought lacrosse was what you find in la church.
   Robin Williams, interview in *Playboy*, 1982

We Bust Ours to Kick Yours
   T-shirt slogan

LACROSSE – LEGALLY BEATING MEN WITH STICKS SINCE 1492
   Bumper sticker, Connecticut

MARATHON, THE

I pulled a hamstring during the New York City Marathon. An hour into the race, I jumped up off the couch.
David Letterman, late-night host

Scratch marathoners once – they tell you how wonderful they feel. Scratch them twice and they tell you about their latest injuries.
Arnold Cooper, American psychiatrist

If you want to know what you'll look like in ten years, look in the mirror after you've run a marathon.
Jeff Scaff, sporting wit

You don't run twenty-six miles at five minutes a mile on good looks and a secret recipe.
Frank Shorter, long-distance runner

I don't really understand miles – I didn't actually know how far it was going to be.
Jade Goody, *Big Brother* celebrity, after failing to complete the 2006 London Marathon

This is a stupid sport, marathon running. Wandering through town, looking for refreshments.
Trina Hess, stand-up comic

See also: ATHLETICS

MIXED MARTIAL ARTS

You can tell by his face that the man is slow – that he is stupid and he has the IQ of a child's shoe size.
   Mirko 'Cro Cop' Filipović, Croatian mixed martial
   artist and former politician of his American opponent,
   Chael Sonnen

You shine like a pagan sun god, you make that whiny prat look foolish, you take their job and you comfort their obviously unsatisfied wife.
   Chael Sonnen

You think I'm cocky? He's for-real cocky. He's like go-to-sleep-praising-himself cocky.
   Rashad Evans, mixed martial artist, hits back at Jon Jones
   after beating Tito Ortiz

It's like the *Titanic* because they've spent a lot of time building him up, but I'm the iceberg.
   Paul Daley, mixed martial artist, before fighting Tyron
   Woodley

See also: BOXING, KARATE

MOTOR RACING

Auto racing is boring except when a car is going at least 172 miles per hour upside down.

Dave Barry, *Miami Herald*

You win some, you lose some, you wreck some.

Dale Earnhardt Jr, American race car driver

Racing is 99 per cent boredom and 1 per cent terror.

Geoff Brabham, Australian racing driver

I want a pit crew... I hate the procedure I currently have to go through when I have car problems.

Dave Barry

Some of the ravines are so deep that if you topple over, your clothes will be out of date by the time you hit the bottom.

Tony Pond, British rally driver, on the dangers of the
Monte Carlo Rally

This guy has been in the grass so often the chipmunks know him by name.

Paul Page, commentator, of Paul Tracy, IndyCar driver

At 180mph, when your front wheel wants to play pogo stick, you don't do nothing. You don't sneeze, you don't hiccup, you don't even breathe. All you do is point it and hang on.

Kenny Roberts, American motorcycle racer

You can always spot a motorcycle racer in a restaurant. He's the one gripping his fork with the first two fingers of his left hand.

Kenny Roberts

It's kind of like tumbling around inside a giant clothes-dryer.

David Aldana, American motorcycle rider, on falling off a
race bike at high speed

I watched the Indy 500 and I was thinking that if they left earlier, they wouldn't have to go so fast.

Steven Wright, comedian

FORMULA 1 MOTOR RACING

The best classroom of all time was about two car lengths behind Juan Manuel Fangio.

Stirling Moss, British racing driver

Once an accident has started happening, you've just got enough time to say 'S***, I'm having a shunt!'

James Hunt, British Formula 1 world champion

Nigel Mansell is so brave, but such a moaner. He should have 'He Who Dares Whines' embroidered on his overalls.

Simon Barnes, *The Times*

In one year I travelled 450,000 miles by air. That's eighteen-and-a-half times around the world, or once around Howard Cosell's head.

Jackie Stewart, Formula 1 world champion

The driver's position will be more horizontal than last year. It will be like lying in a bath with your feet on the taps, but not as comfortable.

David Coulthard, British Formula 1 driver, on Williams-Renault's new design, 1995

In my sport the quick are too often listed among the dead.

Jackie Stewart

I've never seen driving as a sexual thing – I just could never consider it in that light. I think women are interested in the drivers because of the dangers, but some of us are as dull as Old Nick.

Jackie Stewart

Grand Prix driving is like balancing an egg on a spoon while shooting the rapids.

Graham Hill, Formula 1 world champion

Ayrton Senna had an immense number of collisions. And they could not all have been everybody else's fault.

Jackie Stewart

My dad once said that you meet a much nicer class of person there, but I'm not sure.

Damon Hill, British racing driver, son of Graham Hill, on starting from the back of the grid

It's got such a beautifully tight behind, it couldn't have been any other name.

> Sebastian Vettel, Formula 1 world champion, on why he calls his Red Bull 2011 car, 'Kylie'

... someone with about as much charisma as a damp spark plug.

> Alan Hubbard, sports columnist, of Formula 1's Nigel Mansell

GAFFES AND BLOOPERS

The drivers have one foot on the brake, one on the clutch and one on the throttle.

> Bob Varsha, Formula 1 commentator

If Alain Prost wants to catch Ayrton Senna, he'll have to get on his bike.

> James Hunt, British driver and commentator

Murray Walker – British Commentator

And now the boot is on the other Schumacher.

He's obviously gone in for a wheel change. I say 'obviously', because I can't see it.

I don't make mistakes. I make prophecies which immediately turn out to be wrong.

I make no apologies for their absence; I'm sorry that they're not here.

It's not quite a curve. It's straight, actually.

This is an interesting circuit because it has inclines. And not just up but down as well.

... the lead is now 6.9 seconds. In fact it's just under 7 seconds.

A mediocre season for Nelson Piquet as he is now known and always has been.

There is nothing wrong with that car except for the fact that it is on fire.

Alain Prost is in a commanding second position.

And now Jacques Laffitte is as close to Surer as Surer is to Laffitte.

I wonder if Watson is in the relaxed state of mind he's in.

Speaking from memory, I don't know how many points Nelson Piquet has...

Tambay's hopes, which were nil before, are absolutely zero now.

With two laps to go then the action will begin, unless this is the action, which it is.

Mansell is slowing down, taking it easy. Oh no, he isn't. It's a lap record.

The atmosphere is so tense, you could cut it with a cricket
stump.

The lead car is absolutely unique, except for the one behind
it, which is identical.

Once he'd got past the point of no return, there was no
going back.

This would have been Senna's third win in a row, if he had
won the two before.

NEWSPAPERS

I once thought of becoming a political cartoonist because they only have to come up with one idea a day. Then I thought I'd become a sportswriter instead because they don't have to come up with any.

Sam Snead, American golfer

I have known ninety-five of these people when they were living. I've written stories about seventy-three of them. I've had cocktails and drinks with forty-seven of them, and I played golf with twenty-four of them. So I want somebody else to try and go up against that record.

Dan Jenkins, golf writer, during his induction speech into the World Golf Hall of Fame, talking about his fellow members of the Hall, 2012

I always turn to the sports section first. The sports page records people's accomplishments; the front page has nothing but man's failures.

Earl Warren, lawyer and politician

I am here to propose a toast to the sportswriters. It's up to you whether you stand up or not.

Fred Trueman, Yorkshire and England bowler, at a sportswriters' dinner

Sure I know where the press room is. I just look for where they throw the dog meat.

Martina Navratilova, tennis player

I've always said there's a place for the press but they haven't dug it yet.

Tommy Docherty, Scottish football manager

Sportswriters on television have become as common as rats in a drain. Sportswriters should be read and not seen.

Norman Chad, *Sports Illustrated*, 1992

The press can best be compared to haemorrhoids.

Gareth Davies, former Welsh rugby union captain

San Francisco sportswriters describe the baseball scene with all the precision of three-year-old children finger painting on the playroom wall.

Jim Brosnan, pitcher and diarist, *The Long Season*, 1960

There isn't anything on earth as depressing as an old sportswriter.

Ring Lardner, wit and old sportswriter

The capacity of sporting journalists to wax lyrical in the face of the exceptional is matched only by the speed with which they run out of adjectives in doing so.

Derek Malcolm, film critic, *The Guardian*

See also COMMENTATORS AND BROADCASTERS

OLYMPICS

My mum's so pessimistic that if there was an Olympics for pessimism … she wouldn't fancy her chances.
  Nish Kumar, comedian

I took part in the sun-tanning Olympics – I just got bronze.
  Tim Vine, comedian

Here's a good trick: get a job as a judge at the Olympics. Then, if some guy sets a world record, pretend that you didn't see it and go, 'Okay, is everybody ready to start now?'
  Jack Handy, *Saturday Night Live*

The only good thing about the Olympics is the opening and closing ceremony. They do a lovely showbiz job. Otherwise, it's complete nonsense.
  Bernie Ecclestone, Formula 1 boss

The only time our girls looked good in Munich was in the discotheque between nine and eleven every night.
  US Olympic coach, 1972

To be Olympic champion, I am convinced you must choose your parents carefully.
  Per-Olof Astrand, Swedish athletic researcher

Finishing second in the Olympics gets you silver. Finishing second in politics gets you oblivion.

Richard Nixon, American President

At the Olympics in China, every color was represented ... and that was just the drinking water.

Evan Sayet, Jewish-American stand-up

That silver medal at the Olympics, that's something isn't it? You get gold, you've won. You get bronze, 'Well, at least I got something.' But silver is basically saying, 'Of everyone that lost, you were the best. No one lost ahead of you. You are the very best loser.'

Jerry Seinfeld, stand-up comedian and actor

The Olympics. Not a sport but several peculiar sports ... each of which only commands your attention every four years, like a dental appointment.

Dan Jenkins, American sportswriter

Notify Olympics: I can't run. Injury:BroKeN heart RT @ LonaPete RT @eonline Prince Harry is off the market! Sorry, ladies.

Lolo Jones, American Olympic hurdler, 2012, tweet

Italy's in next building. Could hear shouts of joy from open windows when they won... Either that or their espresso machine finally got fixed.

Lolo Jones, 2012, tweet

To celebrate the closing of the Olympics, I invited the swimmers to a pool party... Still no takers.

Lolo Jones, 2012, tweet

I was not talented enough to run and smile at the same time.
  Emile Zatopek, Czechoslovakian runner, when asked to
  explain his strange facial expression while running

Jeremy Hunt has introduced a new sport to the Games, to
go with the discus, shot-put, javelin. It is bell-whanging. He
shows his class on YouTube. The rules have yet to be codified – there is still a dispute about whether you get extra
points for hitting a spectator – but you can be sure they will
be codified in London.
  Boris Johnson, mayor of London in, 'Here's 20 jolly good
  reasons to feel cheerful about the Games', *Daily Telegraph*,
  referring to a moment when the Culture Secretary tried to
  ring a bell with a loose clanger

Drugs are not allowed at the Olympics. Unless you're in
charge of thinking up the opening ceremony, in which case
they're mandatory.
  Alistair Barrie, comedian, Edinburgh Festival, August 2012

I knew the UK would do well at the Olympics because,
thanks to last year's riots, most of our young folk have
sportswear.
  Steve N. Allen, comedian, Edinburgh Festival, August 2012

We did well in the Olympics. We were snatching gold off
other countries like we had an empire again.
  Juliet Meyers, comedienne, Edinburgh Festival, August
  2012

I really hope this win improves my pulling power with
women, if I'm honest! That's about it.
  Scott Brash, Scottish show jumper, after winning gold in 2012

Got all me kit, still think Stella was a bit Lucy in the Sky when she knocked this one up.

Bradley Wiggins, British Olympic gold medallist, cyclist, 2012, reflecting on the Stella McCartney-designed Olympic outfits

After London 2012 I want to go into the press conference before anyone asks me a question, and just say, 'You are now looking at a living legend.'

Usain Bolt, champion sprinter, London 2012

It's really embarrassing but one of the first things that comes up when you type my name into Google is 'Jessica Ennis bum'.

Jessica Ennis, British Olympic gold medallist, heptathlete, 2012

See also: ATHLETICS, MARATHON, TRACK AND FIELD, WINTER SPORTS

PARACHUTING

I went to a parachute-jumping class. The drop-out rate was incredible.
   Anon.

If at first you don't succeed, then maybe skydiving isn't for you.
   Anon.

I was skydiving, horizontally.
   Steven Wright, stand-up

POKER

Poker, n. A game said to be played with cards for some purpose to this lexicographer unknown.
   Ambrose Bierce, *The Devil's Dictionary*, 1911

Poker's a day to learn and a lifetime to master.
   Robert Williamson III, professional poker player

[Poker is] as elaborate a waste of human intelligence as you could find outside an advertising agency.
   Raymond Chandler, novelist

[Poker] exemplifies the worst aspects of capitalism that have made our country so great.
   Walter Matthau, actor

Last night I stayed up late playing poker with Tarot cards. I got a full house and four people died.
   Steven Wright, comedian

Old card players never die, they just shuffle away.
   Anon.

Poker is 100 per cent skill and 50 per cent luck.
   Phil Hellmuth, professional poker player

Your best chance to get a Royal Flush in a casino is in the bathroom.

V. P. Pappy, writer on poker

If you sit down at a poker game and, after twenty minutes, don't see a sucker, get up. You're the sucker.

Anon.

There are few things that are so unpardonably neglected in our country as poker. The upper class knows very little about it. Now and then you find ambassadors who have sort of a general knowledge of the game, but the ignorance of the people is fearful. Why, I have known clergymen, good men, kind-hearted, liberal, sincere, and all that, who did not know the meaning of a 'flush'. It is enough to make one ashamed of the species.

Mark Twain, American author

Is it a reasonable thing, I ask you, for a grown man to run about and hit a ball? Poker's the only game fit for a grown man. Then, your hand is against every man's, and every man's is against yours. Teamwork? Who ever made a fortune by teamwork? There's only one way to make a fortune, and that's to down the fellow who's up against you.

W. Somerset Maugham, novelist

I believe in poker the way I believe in the American Dream. Poker is good for you. It enriches the soul, sharpens the intellect, heals the spirit, and – when played well – nourishes the wallet.

Lou Krieger

POLO

Playing polo is like trying to play golf during an earthquake.
  Sylvester Stallone, actor

Sex – the poor man's polo.
  Clifford Odets, dramatist and screenwriter

Marilyn Monroe: Water polo? Isn't that terribly dangerous?
Tony Curtis: I'll say! I had two ponies drown under me.
  Billy Wilder, *Some Like It Hot*, 1959

REFEREES AND UMPIRES

It's terrible how they treat umpires in the US. When they first go out on the field, the band starts to play, 'Oh Say Can You See?'

Goodman Ace, comedian

The trouble with referees is that they just don't care which side wins.

Tom Canterbury, basketball coach

I occasionally get birthday cards from fans. But it's often the same message: they hope it's my last.

Al Forman, baseball umpire

I was asked to be a linesman at the Wimbledon tennis championships. I excused myself by expressing myself flattered by the offer, but begged them to renew it when my eyesight had deteriorated sufficiently to be able to make wrong decisions with absolute conviction.

Peter Ustinov, actor and raconteur

Ideally, the umpire should combine the integrity of a Supreme Court judge, the physical agility of an acrobat, the endurance of Job and the imperturbability of Buddha.

'The Villains in Blue', *Time* magazine, 1961

I wanted to have a career in sports when I was young, but I had to give it up. I'm only 6 feet tall, so I couldn't play basketball. I'm only 190 pounds, so I couldn't play football. And I have 20–20 vision, so I couldn't be a referee.

Jay Leno, late-night host

It was like the referee had a brand-new yellow card and wanted to see if it worked.

Richard Rufus, Charlton Athletic defender

He can't even control his kids so I wonder how he can control a game of football.

Kay Webb on her husband, Howard, being chosen to referee the World Cup final

It's like a toaster, that shirt pocket. Every time there's a tackle, up pops a yellow card.

Kevin Keegan, player and pundit, of French referee during 1994 World Cup

Another umpire was attacked by a fan. That's not fair. With their poor eyesight, you know, umpires can't pick suspects out of line-ups.

Jay Leno

Now I know why there is only one 'I' in umpire.

Anon.

The NFL broke history today with the first female ref at The Lions game. I was impressed, she didn't take off her heels till the third quarter.

Lolo Jones, American Olympic hurdler, 2012, tweet

Eventually the pool from which stewards were selected was extended beyond the registered blind, the chronically inbred and those whose ear trumpets or searing gout problems rendered them half-sharp or pathologically vicious.

  Alastair Down, on racing stewards

They expect an umpire to be perfect on opening day and to improve as the season goes on.

  Nestor Chylak, Major League Baseball umpire

I never criticise referees and I'm not going to change a habit for that prat.

  Ron Atkinson, manager

If that was a penalty, I'll plait sawdust.

  Ron Atkinson, reacting to a penalty decision against his
  team, Sheffield Wednesday

They are supposed to be dispassionate dispensers of Pure Justice, icy islands of emotionless calculation. In short, umpires should be acute Republicans.

  George F. Will, sportswriter

Trying to maintain order during a legalized gang brawl involving eighty toughs with a little whistle, a hanky and a ton of prayer.

  Anonymous American football referee, explaining his job

What happens to a cricketer when his eyesight starts to fail? He applies to be an umpire.

  Anon.

Steve Bucknor has completely lost the plot. He should take his pension back and sail off to the sunset.

Bob Willis, commentator and former England bowler, on West Indian umpire

The problem with Earl [Weaver] is that he holds a grudge. Other managers, if they disagree with a call, may holler and shout, but you can still go out for a beer with them after the game. Not Earl. He never forgets. Heck, he even holds your minor league record against you. Once, a couple of years ago, I made a controversial call at the plate. Earl charged out of the dugout, screaming that that was the same call I'd blown at Elmira in '66. That sort of thing can get to you.

Ron Luciano, Major League Baseball umpire

Any umpire who lasts five years in the minor leagues deserves to be immortalized. Any umpire who lasts ten or more years in the minors deserves to be institutionalized.

Ron Luciano

The umpires have kept this game honest for 100 years. We're the only segment of the game that has never been touched by scandal. We gotta be too dumb to cheat. We must have integrity, because we sure don't have a normal family life. We certainly aren't properly paid. We have no health care, no job security, no tenure. Our pension plan is a joke. We take more abuse than any living group of humans, and can't give back any. If we're fired without notice, our only recourse is to appeal to the league president. And he's the guy that fires you. That's gotta be unconstitutional.

Ron Luciano

Pity the woman who marries a baseball umpire and has to have a man around the house who is always right.
    Anon.

I can see the sun OK, and that's 93 million miles away.
    Baseball umpire Bruce Froemming, after having his
    eyesight questioned

It ain't nothin' till I call it.
    Bill Klem, the 'father of baseball umpires'

In a way, an umpire is like a woman. He makes quick decisions, never reverses them and doesn't think you're safe when you're out.
    Baseball umpire Larry Goetz

See also: BASEBALL, CRICKET, FOOTBALL

ROWING

Every creature has within him the wild, uncontrollable urge to punt.

Charles Schultz, *Snoopy*

The Oxford rowing crew – eight minds with but one single thought, if that.

Max Beerbohm, English novelist

Ah! Isn't that nice! The wife of the Cambridge president is kissing the cox of the Oxford crew.

Harry Carpenter, BBC commentator at the Boat Race

... and somewhat surprisingly Cambridge have won the toss.

Harry Carpenter

The Oxford–Cambridge Boat Race would be much more attractive if the boats were allowed to ram each other.

Miles Kington, English humorist

RUGBY LEAGUE

In south-west Lancashire, babes don't toddle, they side-step. Queuing women talk of 'nipping round the blindside'. Rugby league provides our cultural adrenalin. It's a physical manifestation of our rules of life: comradeship, honest endeavour, and a staunch, often ponderous allegiance to fair play.

Colin Welland, screenwriter

Not many people in Batley speak Latin, so the first thing we did was change the motto.

Stephen Ball, after taking over as chairman of Batley rugby league club

League is much, much more physical than union, and that's before anyone starts breaking the rules.

Adrian Hadley, Welsh rugby union and rugby league winger

I'm forty-nine, I've had a brain haemorrhage and a triple bypass and I could still go out and play a reasonable game of rugby union. But I wouldn't last thirty seconds in rugby league.

Graham Lowe, New Zealand rugby league coach and administrator

The main difference between playing league and union is that now I get my hangovers on Monday instead of Sunday.
    Tom David, Welsh rugby union and rugby league player

Bradford is famous for sheep, but we didn't think that had quite the same ring. When we asked on local radio for a name with Yorkshire connotations someone suggested puddings. So it's Bulls.
    Peter Deakin, rugby league administrator and promoter, on
    renaming Bradford Northern as the Bulls

To play rugby league, you need three things: a good pass, a good tackle and a good excuse.
    Anon.

GAFFES AND BLOOPERS

I don't want to sit on the fence, but it could go either way.
    Maurice Bamford, rugby league player and coach and
    author

It's Great Britain in the all white strip, with the red and blue V, the dark shorts and dark socks.
    Ray French, dual-code international player

See also: RUGBY UNION

RUGBY UNION

In 1823, William Webb Ellis first picked up the ball in his arms and ran with it. And for the next 156 years forwards have been trying to work out why.

Sir Tasker Watkins, judge and president of the Welsh Rugby Union

RUGBY IS PLAYED BY MEN WITH ODD SHAPED BALLS

Bumper sticker, Bristol

... fifty-seven old farts.

Will Carling, England captain, describing the executive of the Rugby Football Union

Jack Rowell has the acerbic wit of Dorothy Parker and, according to most New Zealanders, a similar knowledge of rugby.

Mark Reason, sports journalist, of Bath and England coach

Once rugby players have succeeded in getting their boots on the right feet, the mental challenge of the game is largely over.

Derek Robinson, English novelist

His air was that of a man who has been passed through a wringer, and his eyes, what you could see of them, had a strange, smouldering gleam. He was so encrusted with alluvial deposits that one realised how little a mere bath would ever be able to effect. To fit him to take his place in polite society, he would certainly have to be sent to the cleaner's. Indeed, it was a moot point whether it wouldn't be simpler just to throw him away.

P. G. Wodehouse, *Very Good, Jeeves*, 1930

I'm not happy with our tackling. We're hurting them, but they keep getting up.

Jimmy Murphy, Irish rugby player and coach

Rugby football is a game I can't claim absolutely to understand in all its niceties, if you know what I mean. I can follow the broad, general principles, of course. I mean to say, I know that the main scheme is to work the ball down the field somehow and deposit it over the line at the other end, and that, in order to squelch this programme, each side is allowed to put in a certain amount of assault and battery and do things to its fellow-man which, if done elsewhere, would result in fourteen days without the option, coupled with some strong remarks from the Bench.

P. G. Wodehouse, *Very Good, Jeeves*, 1930

Beer and rugby are more or less synonymous.

Chris Laidlaw, All Black, diplomat, MP, radio host and author, 1973

We were so fired up, when the referee ran on to the pitch, three of us tackled him.

Graham Dawe, Plymouth Albion player and coach

If I had been a winger, I might have been daydreaming and thinking about how to keep my kit clean for next week.
  Bill Beaumont, England captain and commentator

Rugby backs can be identified because they generally have clean jerseys and identifiable partings in their hair... Come the revolution the backs will be the first to be lined up against the wall and shot for living parasitically off the work of others.
  Peter FitzSimons, Australian player and journalist

Forwards are the gnarled and scarred creatures who have a propensity for running into and bleeding all over each other.
  Peter FitzSimons

The winger resembles Mother Brown, running with a high knee-lift and sometimes not progressing far from the spot where he started.
  Mark Reason, *Total Sport*, 1996, on Irishman Simon
  Geoghegan

The Brent Spar with attitude. A figure who inspires hero worship among even those who think a fly-half is a glass of beer consumed when 'er indoors is looking the other way.
  Robert Philip, *Daily Telegraph*, on All Black Jonah Lomu

Believe me, if you've played an hour and a half of rugby and you've really enjoyed it, you're not going to want to go off and get involved in some gang fight.
  Boris Johnson, mayor of London, on a rugby playing initia-
  tive for young men

I think Brian Moore's gnashers are the kind you get from a DIY shop and hammer in yourself.

Paul Rendall, player and coach

Richie McCaw can eat a Weetabix in fifteen seconds dry. Two minutes later I am still chewing it. That's probably the difference between us.

James Haskell, England player, of the All Black captain

If you can't take a punch, you should play table tennis.

Pierre Berbizier, French rugby union player and coach, following Scotland's accusations of French foul play

A major rugby tour by the British Isles to New Zealand is a cross between a mediaeval crusade and a prep school outing.

John Hopkins, rugby author

Tony Ward is the most important rugby player in Ireland. His legs are far more important to his country than even those of Marlene Dietrich were to the film industry. A little hairier, maybe, but a pair of absolute winners.

Mike Gibson, Wales vs. Ireland match programme, 1979

No leadership, no ideas. Not even enough imagination to thump someone in the line-out when the ref wasn't looking.

J. P. R. Williams, former Welsh player, on Wales losing 28–9 against Australia

The relationship between the Welsh and the English is based on trust and understanding. They don't trust us and we don't understand them.

Dudley Wood, rugby union administrator

The Holy Writ of Gloucester Rugby Club demands: first, that the forwards shall win the ball; second, that the forwards shall keep the ball; and third, the backs shall buy the beer.

Doug Ibbotson, sportswriter, *Daily Telegraph*

I've seen better centres in a box of Black Magic.

Joe McPartlin, on his successors in the Oxford University backs

Colin Meads is the kind of player you expect to see emerging from a ruck with the remains of a jockstrap between his teeth.

Tom O'Reilly, rugby writer, of New Zealand rugby union international

A bomb under the west car park at Twickenham on an international day would end fascism in England for a generation.

Philip Toynbee, British writer and communist

Modern rugby players like to get their retaliation in first.

Kim Fletcher, sportswriter

You've got to get your first tackle in early, even if it's late.

Ray Gravell, Welsh international

In my time, I've had my knee out, broken my collarbone, had my nose smashed, a rib broken, lost a few teeth, and ricked my back; but as soon as I get a bit of bad luck I'm going to quit the game.

J. W. Robinson

Look what these bastards have done to Wales. They've taken our coal, our water, our steel. They buy our houses and they only live in them for a fortnight every twelve months. What have they given us? Absolutely nothing. We've been exploited, raped, controlled and punished by the English – and that's who you are playing this afternoon.

> Phil Bennett in a team talk before facing England in 1979

Nobody ever beats Wales at rugby, they just score more points.

> Graham Mourie, New Zealand player and coach

Every time I went to tackle him, Horrocks went one way, Taylor went the other, and all I got was the bloody hyphen.

> Nick England on trying to stop Phil Horrocks-Taylor,
> England fly-half

I've done stupid things before when I've had too many sherbets but nothing like this.

> Andy Powell, Welsh forward, after his arrest for driving a
> golf buggy down the M4 while over the alcohol limit

I'm disappointed because we could have won, but as Mr Winston Churchill said, success is the ability to go from one failure to another with no loss of enthusiasm.

> Marc Lièvremont, France coach, following their Six
> Nations defeat at Twickenham, 2011

GAFFES AND BLOOPERS

Dusty Hare kicked nineteen out of the seventeen points.

> David Coleman, BBC commentator

If you didn't know him, you wouldn't know who he was.
  Nigel Starmer-Smith, commentator

A pressure kick for Andrew with Brown breathing down his throat.
  Nigel Starmer-Smith

It shows what a hot seat that number-9 jersey has been.
  Nigel Starmer-Smith

He's like a needle in a haystack, this man – he's everywhere.
  Ray French, rugby union and rugby league dual-code
  international and commentator

He scored that try after only twenty-two seconds – totally against the run of play.
  Murray Mexted, New Zealand captain and commentator

An easy kick for George Fairbairn now but, as everybody knows, no kicks are easy.
  David Doyle-Davidson, player and coach

That could have made it 10–3 and there's a subtle difference between that and 7–3.
  Bill McLaren, Scottish commentator

See also: RUGBY LEAGUE

SAILING

He not only lied about the size of his boat, he made me row it.
    Anon.

The day a man buys a boat is the second happiest day of his life. The happiest day, of course, is the day he sells it.
    Anon.

There isn't a record in existence that hasn't been broken.
    Chay Blyth, round-the-world yachtsman

Ocean Racing is like standing under a cold shower in a howling gale tearing up twenty-pound notes.
    Edward Heath, yachtsman and former British Prime Minister

SKIING

Skiing? Why break my leg at forty degrees below zero, when I can fall downstairs at home?
  Corey Ford, American humorist and author

Why does there have to be a style judge for the ski jump which is, to the unpractised eye, simply controlled falling from a tenth-storey window?
  A. A. Gill, *Sunday Times*

There are two main forms of this sport: Alpine skiing and Nordic skiing. Alpine skiing involves a mountain and a $5,000 to $10,000 minimum investment, plus $300,000 for the condo in Aspen and however much you spend on drugs. It is a sport only a handful of people ever master, and those who do, do so at the expense of other skills like talking and writing their own name.
  National Lampoon, 1979

Skiers view snowboarders as a menace; snowboarders view skiers as Elmer Fudd.
  Dave Barry, *Miami Herald*

The sport of skiing consists of wearing three thousand dollars' worth of clothes and equipment and driving two hundred miles in the snow in order to stand around at a bar and get drunk.

P. J. O'Rourke, *Modern Manners*, 1983

The only interesting part of skiing is seeing someone crash. Violently.

Denis Leary, writer and comedian

Snowboarding is an activity that is very popular with people who do not feel that regular skiing is lethal enough.

Dave Barry

If you ever see any blacks or Mexicans on top of a snow-capped mountain, call 911. There's been a plane accident.

Paul Rodriguez, Mexican-born American stand-up

Skiing is the only sport where you can spend an arm and a leg to break an arm and a leg.

Henry Beard, *Skiing*, 1989

Skiing combines outdoor fun with knocking down trees with your face.

Dave Barry

Skiing is easy. I learned in just ten sittings.

Anon.

Stretch pants – the garment that made skiing a spectator sport.

Anon.

Skiing? I do not participate in any sport that has ambulances at the bottom of the hill.
  Erma Bombeck, humorous writer

I went skiing last week and broke a leg. Fortunately, it wasn't mine.
  Anon.

Cross-country skiing is great if you live in a small country.
  Steven Wright, comedian

St Moritz, the heart of the broken-limb country, where a man must prove himself first on skis and then on a stretcher.
  Art Buchwald, *I Chose Caviar*, 1957

See also: WINTER SPORTS, ICE HOCKEY

SNOOKER

Whoever called snooker 'chess with balls' was rude, but right.
  Clive James, *Daily Telegraph*, 2012

Two-piece snooker cues are popular these days, but Alex Higgins doesn't use one because there aren't any instructions.
  Steve Davis, commentator

His natural expression is that of a man who may have mislaid his winning lottery ticket.
  Paul Weaver of Welsh player Matthew Stevens

He reached new levels of stupidity, even by his own cretinous standards.
  John Rawling, journalist, of Australian Quinten Hann

I remember when Steve Davis used to take Valium as a stimulant.
  Dennis Taylor, Northern Irish player, of rival

Ronnie O'Sullivan's wild looks and wilder behaviour suggest he may be the Gallagher brother Liam and Noel threw out of Oasis for being too unstable.
  Matthew Norman, journalist

I played snooker like a pig with a shotgun.
   Mark Williams, Welsh snooker player

Dressing a pool player in a tuxedo is like putting whipped cream on a hot dog.
   Minnesota Fats, pool legend

I have never liked working. To me a job is an invasion of privacy.
   Daniel McGoorty, acclaimed billiards hustler

Bums play pool, gentlemen play billiards.
   Daniel McGoorty

When I realised that what I had turned out to be was a lousy, two-bit pool hustler and drunk, I wasn't depressed at all, I was glad to have a profession.
   Daniel McGoorty

GAFFES AND BLOOPERS

And now snooker, and Steve Davis has crashed out of the UK Billiards Championship.
   Allan Taylor

I like playing in Sheffield, it's full of melancholy happy-go-lucky people.
   Alex Higgins

Now that cue arm, now in perfect rhythm with his thinking.
John Pulman

Well it seems at the moment as if the pockets are as big as goal posts for Willie Thorne.
John Pulman

He's obviously worked out for himself that he doesn't need that last red, great thinker this man.
Dennis Taylor

Tony Meo beginning to find his potting boots.
Rex Williams

From this position you've got to fancy either yourself or your opponent winning.
Kirk Stevens

This said, the inevitable failed to happen.
John Pulman

He'll have no trouble in solving the solution.
Jack Karnehm, snooker commentator

Well, valour was the better part of discretion there.
Jack Karnehm

Sometimes the deciding frame is always the hardest one to win.
Dennis Taylor

David Vine – BBC Commentator

10–4 – and it could mean exactly what it means.

But there was the big prize money hanging there, like a carrot waiting to be picked.

Here we are in the Holy Land of Israel, a Mecca for tourists.

No one came closer to winning the world title last year than the runner-up Dennis Taylor.

Suddenly Alex Higgins was 7–0 down.

This match has gradually and suddenly come to a climax.

Ray Reardon, one of the great Crucible champions, won it five times, when the championship was played away from the Crucible.

After twelve frames they stand all square. The next frame, believe it or not, is the thirteenth.

Ted Lowe – BBC Commentator

And Alex Higgins has literally come back from the dead.

And for those of you watching this in black and white, the pink sits behind the yellow.

And it is my guess that Steve Davis will try to score as many points as he can in this frame.

And Jimmy's potting is literally doing the commentary here.

He's lucky in one sense and lucky in the other.

Higgins first entered the championship ten years ago, that was for the first time, of course.

Steve Davis has a tough consignment in front of him.

All square all the way round.

Can Bill Werbeniuk be the second Canadian to rewrite the history books?

This young man Jimmy White celebrated his twenty-second birthday literally four days ago.

And Griffiths has looked at that blue four times now, and it still hasn't moved.

The formalities are now over and it's down to business, Steve Davis now adjusting his socks.

Steve, with his sip of water, part of his make-up.

And that's the third time he's done that this session. He's missed his waistcoat pocket with the chalk.

Cliff Thorburn has been unsettled by the erratic but consistent potting of Perrie Mans.

Fred Davis, the doyen of snooker, now sixty-seven years of age and too old to get his leg over, prefers to use his left hand.

He's completely disappeared. He's gone back to his dressing-room. Nobody knows where he has gone.

It all adds up to a bit of fun. If commentators can't join in with the rest of the world, they must cry alone.

Jimmy can make these balls talk – and what a story they are telling.

Jimmy White has that wonderful gift of being able to point his cue where he is looking.

John Smyth [the referee] is getting his little implement out.

Of course, one of Stephen Hendry's greatest assets is his ability to score when he's playing.

Oh, and that's a brilliant shot. The odd thing is, his mum's not very keen on snooker.

That puts the game beyond reproach.

That's inches away from being millimetre-perfect.

The audience are literally electrified and glued to their seats.

The audience is standing to relieve themselves.

There is, I believe, a time limit for playing a shot. But I think it's true to say that nobody knows what that limit is.

SPORT

Sport is the only entertainment where, no matter how many times you go back, you never know the ending.
  Neil Simon, playwright

Have you noticed that whatever sport you're trying to learn, some earnest person is always telling you to keep your knees bent?
  Dave Barry, *Miami Herald*

Life without sports is like life without underpants.
  Billy Bowden, New Zealand cricketer and umpire

Mankind's yearning to engage in sports is older than recorded history, dating back to the time millions of years ago, when the first primitive man picked up a crude club and a round rock, tossed the rock into the air, and whomped the club into the sloping forehead of the first primitive umpire.
  Dave Barry

What inner force drove this first athlete? Your guess is as good as mine. Better, probably, because you haven't had four beers.
  Dave Barry

I detest games – I never like to kick or be kicked.
  Oscar Wilde, playwright

Good sports are rarely good at sports.
  Sally Poplin, humorous writer

The more violent the body contact of the sports you watch, the lower the class.
  Paul Fussell, historian

Practically every game played internationally today was invented in Britain, and when foreigners become good enough to match, or even defeat, the British, the British quickly invented a new game.
  Peter Ustinov, actor and anecdotalist

Every sport pretends to a literature, but people don't believe it of any other sport but their own.
  Alistair Cooke, broadcaster

When it comes to sports I am not particularly interested. Generally speaking, I look upon them as dangerous and tiring activities performed by people with whom I share nothing except the right to trial by jury.
  Fran Lebowitz, *Metropolitan Life*, 1978

In America it is sport that is the opiate of the masses.
  Russell Baker, *New York Times*, 1967

I hate sports as rabidly as a person who likes sports hates common sense.
  H. L. Mencken, wit

The invention of the ball was one of the worst tragedies ever to befall mankind and to force small boys on to soggy playing fields every afternoon to kick or throw or hurl these objects to each other for a couple of hours before returning the ball to precisely where they had first found it is a near criminal waste of time, energy and childhood.

Robert Morley, actor and wit

Serious sport has nothing to do with fair play. It is bound up with hatred, jealousy, boastfulness, disregard of all rules and sadistic pleasure in witnessing violence: in other words it is war minus the shooting.

George Orwell, 'The Sporting Spirit', *Tribune*, 1945

Son, when you participate in sporting events, it's not whether you win or lose, it's how drunk you get.

Homer Simpson, sage

He's long ago given up hope of finding a country anywhere in the world where it was safe to tell total strangers that he had no interest in sports whatsoever.

Greg Egan, *Zendegi*, 2010

Games are the last resort of those who do not know how to idle.

Robert Lynd, essayist

I am getting to an age when I can only enjoy the last sport left. It is called hunting for your spectacles.

Lord Grey, 1927

SURFING

When you're surfing, you're living. Everything else is just waiting.
   Josh Mitchell

I tried body surfing once, but how often do you find a corpse?
   Emo Philips, stand-up

SWIMMING

If swimming is so good for your figure, how come whales look the way they do?
    Anon.

If one synchronised swimmer drowns, do all the rest have to drown too?
    Steven Wright, comedian

Where did you learn to swim?
In the water.
    Anon.

Chlorine: The Breakfast of Champions!
    T-shirt slogan, Weston-super-Mare, 2008

Greenslade: Ten miles he swam – the last three were agony.
Seagoon: They were over land. Finally I fell in a heap on the ground. I've no idea who left it there.
    Spike Milligan, *The Goon Show*, 1954

I thought I could trust the people who use my pool, but all I know is that when I filled it last year, I put in 10,000 gallons and when I emptied it last week, I took out 11,000 gallons.
    Anon.

I used to use taffy, but it took too long to chew. So did liquorice. But I can take gumdrops to the side of the pool and drop them in the swimmers' mouths, and they won't miss very much practice time.

Donna Maiello, swimming coach at Carnegie-Mellon University, on why she feeds her swimmers gumdrops as a reward for good practices

I wanted to be an Olympic swimmer but I had some problems with buoyancy.

Woody Allen, comedian

I'm even competitive when I drive. I like to beat my sat-nav.

Rebecca Adlington, British Olympic gold-medal-winning freestyle swimmer

What I have never been able to discover is whether the fellows who swim the Channel are obliged to keep their feet off the ground all the way.

E. V. Knox, *It Occurs to Me*, 1926

TABLE TENNIS

It is hard to think of a single Chinese sport at the Olympics, compared with umpteen invented by Britain, including ping-pong, I'll have you know, which originated at upper-class dinner tables and was first called whiff-whaff.

Boris Johnson, mayor of London, *Have I Got Views for You*, 2006

Q: How many ping-pong players does it take to change a light bulb?

A: Four. One to complain that it's 'table tennis' not 'ping-pong', one to change the light bulb, one to protest about the type of glue he used to fix the light bulb into place, and one to get out his copy of the 'Bats "R" Us' catalogue and point out that he could have bought an even better one for 50p less. Anon.

TELEVISION

Men forget everything; women remember everything. That's why men need instant replays in sports. They've already forgotten what happened.

Rita Rudner, comedienne

A rabid sports fan is one that boos a TV set.

Jimmy Cannon, American sportswriter

See also: COMMENTATORS AND BROADCASTERS

TENNIS

No one is more serious about his game than a weekend tennis player.

Jimmy Cannon, sports journalist

I play Cinderella tennis. That is I don't quite get to the ball.

Larry Adler, Anglo-American entertainer

The worst thing I ever said to a tennis umpire was, 'Are you sure?'

Rod Laver, Australian champion

If you see a tennis player who looks as if he is working hard, that means he isn't very good.

Helen Wills Moody, champion tennis player

Tennis is a young man's game. Until you're twenty-five, you can play singles. From twenty-five to thirty-five, you should play doubles. I won't tell you exactly how old I am, but when I played, there were twenty-eight men on the court – just on my side of the net.

George Burns, comedian

I play tennis and I'm pretty good, but no matter how much I practise, I'll never be as good as a wall.

Mitch Hedberg, stand-up

In lawn tennis mixed, the basic chivalry move is to pretend to serve less fiercely to the woman than to the man. This is particularly useful if your first service tends to be out in any case.

Stephen Potter, *Lifemanship*, 1950

Andrea Jaeger plays tennis like she's double-parked.

Mary Carillo, tennis player and sportscaster

I have finally mastered what to do with the second tennis ball. Having small hands, I was becoming terribly self-conscious about keeping it in a can in the car while I served the first one. I noted some women tucked the second ball just inside the elastic leg of their tennis panties. I tried, but found the space already occupied by a leg. Now, I simply drop the second ball down my cleavage, giving me a chest that often stuns my opponent throughout an entire set.

Erma Brombeck, comic writer

Pavarotti is very difficult to pass at the net in tennis, with or without a racquet.

Peter Ustinov, actor and raconteur

During the warming-up training before play I prayed. Not for victory, but that my hairpiece wouldn't fall off.

Andre Agassi, tennis player

I knew it was OK to die after the Wimbledon final but not during it. It would have put Goran off.

Srdjan Ivanisevic, father of Goran, describing problems with his heart during a Wimbledon final

The one fool-proof way of putting the ticket touts out of business – a Wimbledon final between Pete Sampras and Jim Courier.

> *The Guardian*, 1993

Steffi Grief ... the unstoppable juggernaut of women's tennis, has just been run over by a Lori.

> *The Sun*, 1994, on Steffi Graf's first round defeat at
> Wimbledon by Lori McNeil

All that's left for me to do is go find John Lloyd and start a family.

> Pam Shriver, player and broadcaster, after an early singles
> exit at Wimbledon

An otherwise happily married couple may turn a mixed doubles game into a scene from *Who's Afraid of Virginia Woolf?*

> Rod Laver

He plays tennis so badly that his opening serve is match point!

> Anon.

They also serve who only stand and wait – unless they're playing tennis.

> Anon.

Met the Queen of England today ... she said she loved me in the *American Pie* movies.

> Andy Roddick tweet from Wimbledon, 2010, part 1

Just so we are clear.... she did not say that ... it was an attempt at humor ... didn't think that was gonna get taken seriously.
   Andy Roddick tweet from Wimbledon, 2010, part 2 – an
   hour later

Just got back from my friend's funeral. He died after being hit on the head by a tennis ball.
It was a lovely service.
   Anon.

To err is human.
To blame it on someone else is doubles.
   Anon.

I can cry like Roger. It's just a shame I can't play like him.
   Andy Murray, after losing to Roger Federer in the
   Australian Open final

If you believe that, I've never questioned a call in my life.
   John McEnroe, on Anna Kournikova's claim that she was
   a virgin

What a polite game tennis is. The chief word in it seems to be 'sorry' and admiration of each other's play crosses the net as frequently as the ball.
   J. M. Barrie, author and dramatist

'Good shot', 'bad luck' and 'Hell' are the five basic words to be used in tennis.
   Virginia Graham, *Say Please*, 1949

Another play is the rearrange-the-string number. Never take the rap for a bad return or no return. Whenever you hit a ball into the net, or miss it entirely, bring the game to a grinding halt by checking the strings of your racket, spending sometimes as much as five minutes separating them and testing their strength. This absolves you of any of the responsibility for a bad shot.

> Erma Bombeck, *If Life is a Bowl of Cherries – What am I Doing in the Pits?*, 1978

No doubt about it ... every day in every way, my game grows stronger. I saw one enthusiast the other day playing with his racket out of the press. I'll have to try that.

> Erma Bombeck

I can't cook ... I can't skate. I'm not perfect.

> Roger Federer, tennis champion, when asked if there is anything he's not good at

Thank you for inventing sushi. I love it.

> Milos Raonic, Canadian tennis player's remarks after winning the Japan Open

We don't come in and think every day, 'How can we bugger up British tennis today?'

> Roger Draper, chief executive of the Lawn Tennis Association, reacting to criticism

Never discuss love with a tennis player, it means nothing to them.

> Anon.

Men hate to lose. I beat my husband once at tennis. I asked him, 'Will we ever make love again?' He said, 'Yes ... but not with each other.'

    Rita Rudner

Anybody who can dial a telephone can master tennis scoring in about fifteen minutes.

    Sally Poplin, humorous writer

Ladies, here's a hint. If you're up against a girl with big boobs, bring her to the net and make her hit backhand volleys. That's the hardest shot for the well-endowed.

    Billie Jean King

Monica Seles. I'd hate to be next door to her on her wedding night.

    Peter Ustinov

When I was forty, my doctor advised me that a man in his forties shouldn't play tennis. I heeded his advice carefully and could hardly wait until I reached fifty to start again.

    Hugo L. Black, politician and jurist

The constant plucking of his racket strings makes him look like a shuffling madman playing a tiny magic harp that only he can hear.

    The Guardian, of Lleyton Hewitt

Imagine the love child of Jimmy Connors and the young Mike Tyson.

    Matthew Norman, journalist, of Lleyton Hewitt

Lindsay Davenport has the turning circle of a station wagon.
Mike Dickson, sportswriter

She sounds like a live pig being slaughtered.
Frew McMillan, South African, of Maria Sharapova's serving grunts

Have you heard of that part of the body called a spine? Get one!
Andy Roddick, to an umpire

Umpiring – the only job in the world where you can screw up on a daily basis and still have one.
Andy Roddick

It's all your fault – but nothing personal.
Andy Roddick, to an umpire

The only thing faster in women's tennis than Venus Williams's serve is Anna Kournikova's exit.
Alan Ray, wit

Michael Chang has all the fire and passion of a public service announcement.
Alix Ramsay, sportswriter

Charlie Pasarell moves so slowly between points that, at times, he seems to be flirting with reverse gear.
Rex Bellamy, *The Times*

Is tennis the oldest game in recorded history?
Well, it was written that Moses served in the Egyptian court.
Anon.

Though your game is hardly the best,
You can fray your opponent's nerves
By methodically bouncing the ball
At least ten times before your serves.
   Arnold J. Zarett, American poet

In tennis the addict moves about a hard rectangle and seeks to ambush a fuzzy ball with a modified snow-shoe.
   Elliott Chaze, journalist

Dad, did they name the shoe after you, or were you named after the shoe?
   Trevor Smith, on Stan Smith's personalised Adidas footwear

Roscoe Tanner seems to have found a way of making his service go even faster, so that the ball is now quite invisible, like Stealth, the American supersonic bomber which nobody has ever seen.
   Clive James, TV critic

INDIVIDUAL TENNIS PLAYERS

Andre Agassi

Being Number Two sucks.
   Andre Agassi

I can't believe how hard Agassi hits the ball. It's like he's got a gun. No one hit the ball like that in my day. Ion Tiriac didn't drive that fast.
   Ilie Nastase

Björn Borg

If Borg's parents hadn't liked the name, he might never have been Björn.

American comic

Bjoring Borg ... a Volvo among tennis stars.

Peter Freedman, *Glad to be Grey*, 1985

Like a Volvo, Björn Borg is rugged, has good after-sales service, and is very dull.

Clive James

Jimmy Connors

I remember when Jimmy and I went into confession and he came out a half-hour later and I said, 'How'd it go?' He said, 'I wasn't finished. The priest said come back next Sunday.'

Chris Evert on Jimmy Connors

Jimmy Connors is loud, aggressive and with the face and hairstyle of a mediaeval varlet; he personifies a generation which tips its hat to no one.

Ian Wooldridge, English sportswriter

John McEnroe

... a walking, talking, screaming, squawking metaphor for What's Wrong With Young People Today.

Julie Burchill, columnist, of John McEnroe

The Benson and Hedges Cup was won by McEnroe ... he was as charming as always, which means that he was as charming as a dead mouse in a loaf of bread.

Clive James

John McEnroe looks as if he is serving round the edge of an imaginary building.

Clive James

... hair like badly turned broccoli.

Clive James

For two weeks I've been seeing the ball like a basketball. Today, I couldn't see it.

Jimmy Connors, on losing badly to John McEnroe
at Wimbledon

John McEnroe's so good. Against him, all you can do is shake hands and take a shower.

Tomáš Šmid, Czech tennis player

What other problems do you have besides being unemployed, a moron and a dork?

John McEnroe, to a spectator

You can't see as well as these f***ing flowers – and they're f***ing plastic!

John McEnroe, to a line judge

Did you win a lottery to be linesman?

John McEnroe

Ivan Lendl

Ivan Lendl's never going to be a great player on grass. The only time he comes to the net is to shake your hand.

Goran Ivanisevic, Croatian tennis player

Ivan Lendl is a robot, a solitary, mechanical man who lives with his dogs behind towering walls at his estate in Connecticut. A man who so badly wants to have a more human image that he's having surgery to remove the bolts from his neck.

Tony Kornheiser, *Washington Post*

Sure, on a given day I could beat him. But it would have to be a day he had food poisoning.

Mel Purcell, American tennis player, after losing to Ivan Lendl in under an hour

Ilie Nastase

Nastase is a Hamlet who wants to play a clown. He is no good at it... Nastase rarely grins and bears it. More commonly he grins, groans, shrugs, slumps, spins around, shakes his head, puffs out his cheeks, rolls on the ground and bears it. Even more common, he does all that and doesn't bear it.

Clive James

I feel like dog trainer who teach dog manners and graces and just when you think dog knows how should act with nice qualities, dog make big puddle and all is wasted.

Ion Tiriac, on being Ilie Nastase's coach

Nastase doesn't have a brain. He has a bird fluttering around in his head.

    Ion Tiriac

Martina Navratilova

How to shake hands.

    Bettina Bunge, on being asked what she had learned after a
    number of quick defeats to Martina

Martina's like the old Green Bay Packers. You know exactly what she's going to do but there isn't a thing you can do about it.

    Arthur Ashe

I just try to concentrate on concentrating.

    Martina Navratilova, on the secret of her success

You can be the best ball striker there is. But if you can't get to the ball, it doesn't matter.

    Martina Navratilova

Pete Sampras

Pete Sampras does have a weakness. He can't cook for a start.

    Michael Chang

Sampras, Sampras, Sampras, Sampras and Sampras.

    Andre Agassi, when asked to name the five best tennis
    players of all time

GAFFES AND BLOOPERS

You can almost hear the silence as they battle it out.
Dan Maskell, BBC commentator

Strangely enough, Kathy Jordan is getting to the net first, which she always does.
Fred Perry, British tennis champion

Lendl has remained throughout as calm as the proverbial iceberg.
Dan Maskell

When Martina is tense, it helps her relax.
Dan Maskell

It's quite clear that Virginia Wade is thriving on the pressure now that the pressure on her to do well is off.
Harry Carpenter, BBC commentator

The Gullikson twins here. An interesting pair, both from Wisconsin.
Dan Maskell

And here's Živojinović, 6 feet 6 inches tall and 14 pounds 10 ounces.
Dan Maskell

McEnroe has got to sit down and work out where he stands.
Fred Perry

We haven't had any more rain since it stopped raining.
Harry Carpenter

Ann's got to take her nerve by the horns.
  Virginia Wade, player and commentator

These ball boys are marvellous. You don't even notice them.
There's a left handed one over there. I noticed him earlier.
  Max Robertson

Martina, she's got several layers of steel out there, like a cat
with nine lives.
  Virginia Wade

If she gets the jitters now, then she isn't the great champion
that she is.
  Max Robertson, BBC commentator

Billie Jean King, with the look on her face that says she can't
believe it ... because she never believes it, and yet, somehow,
I think she does.
  Max Robertson

Diane – keeping her head beautifully on her shoulders.
  Ann Jones, player and commentator

... and when Chrissie is playing well I always feel that she
is playing well.
  Ann Jones

Živojinović seems to be able to pull the big bullet out of the
top drawer.
  Mike Ingham, commentator

He's got his hands on his knees and holds his head in despair.
  Peter Jones, commentator

Those two volleys, really could be the story of this match summed up at the end of it.

Barry Davies, BBC commentator

This is the third week the fish seem to be getting away from British tennis players.

Gerald Williams, commentator

TENPIN BOWLING

The bowling alley is the poor man's country club.
Sanford Hansell, American wit

One advantage of golf over bowling is that you never lose a bowling ball.
Don Carter

Bowling is a sport that should be right down your alley.
Anon.

I bowled for two years in college because I was drunk and I needed shoes.
Kathleen Madigan, stand-up

In the Bowling Alley of Tomorrow, there will even be machines that wear rental shoes and throw the ball for you. Your sole function will be to drink beer.
Dave Barry, *Miami Herald*

I like to go to the bowling alley and bring a little black marble with me, and put it inside that machine that they use to polish the balls. And then I call the manager over.
James Leemer, actor and comedian

According to a recent study, the most popular fitness sport among Americans is bowling. Is this really a 'fitness' sport? Any sport where you can drink beer and eat pizza while you're doing the sport is not a sport.

Jay Leno, late-night host

See also: BOWLS

TRACK AND FIELD

Mention that you are a hammer thrower to someone who is not an athletics enthusiast and you will be met with any reaction from a puzzled frown to raucous laughter. If you have the misfortune to say it to a groundsman, you may face physical violence.

    Howard Payne, British Olympic hammer thrower

Watching the Russian female shot-putters is like watching an eighteen-stone ballet dancer.

    David Campbell, British athlete

I always wanted to be a minor poet. I remember when I did my record long jump saying to myself, when I was in the air half-way, 'This may be pretty good jumping. It's dashed poor minor poetry!'

    C. B. Fry, English polymath, sportsman, cricketer, diplomat,
    politician, poet

He finally got a place in the Great British team for the Olympics – as a javelin-catcher.

    Anon.

I came first in the limbo competition. Or, as they put it, last in the high jump.

    Milton Jones, comedian

My first 18-foot pole vault wasn't any more of a thrill than my first clearance at 15- or 16- or 17-foot. I just had more time to enjoy it on the way down.

Roland Carter, American pole-vaulter

I don't think the discus will ever attract any interest until they let us start throwing them at one another.

Al Oerter, American discus thrower

If this new method is accepted I will personally break my javelin in half and use it as a support for my tomato plants.

Dana Zátopková, Czech athlete, on news of a new throwing style

Plainly no way has yet been found to stop long-jump commentaries sounding like naughty stories after lights-out in the dorm – 'Ooooh! It's enormous. It was *so* long!'

Russell Davies, *Sunday Times*

I know I'm no Kim Basinger, but she can't throw a javelin.

Fatima Whitbread, English athlete

People think of me as the Incredible Hulk.

Fatima Whitbread

I come from a very athletic family. My brother once broke a leg throwing a ball. He forgot it was chained to his ankle.

Anon.

See also: ATHLETICS

WATERSKIING

I got a pair of waterskis for my birthday. All I need now is a lake with a slope.

Anon.

All things are possible, except for skiing through a revolving door.

Anon.

The problem with waterskiing is the risk of a 30mph enema.

Anon.

WINNING AND LOSING

I'm now a living legend. Bask in my glory!
> Usain Bolt, after becoming the first man to win the
> Olympic 100m and 200m sprint double twice in
> succession, 2012

Show me a good and gracious loser and I'll show you
a failure.
> Knute Rockne, Notre Dame football coach

Losing is the great American sin.
> John Tunis, writer of sports fiction, quoted in the *New
> York Times*, 1977

Nobody remembers who finished second but the guy who
finished second.
> Bobby Unser, Indianapolis 500 driver

There's only one man allowed to say, 'There's nothing wrong
with defeat', and that's Nelson Mandela's chiropodist.
> Jack Powell, Major League Baseball pitcher

In top-class sport, you're the rooster one day, just a feather
duster the next.
> Alan Jones, Australian rugby player, coach and broadcaster

Victory goes to the player who makes the next-to-last mistake.
Jackie Mason, comedian

It's not whether you win or lose but how you place the blame.
Sally Poplin, humorous writer

If you don't believe you can win, there is no point in getting out of bed at the end of the day.
Neville Southall, Welsh goalkeeper

Anybody can win. Unless there happens to be a second entry.
George Ade, columnist and playwright

No one ever says 'It's only a game' when their team is winning.
Anon.

[handwritten: JOHN 07 967486 769]

Whoever said, It's not whether you win or lose that counts ... probably lost.
Martina Navratilova, tennis player

My only feeling about superstition is that it's unlucky to be behind at the end of the game.
Duffy Daugherty, football player and coach of Michigan State University

A tie is like kissing your sister.
Duffy Daugherty

Of course I want to win it... I'm not here to have a good time, nor to keep warm and dry.
Nick Faldo, golfer, while leading the field at the PGA golf championship, 1996

Sure, winning isn't everything. It's the only thing.
    Henry 'Red' Sanders, American football player and coach,
    Sports Illustrated, 1955

Winning is like shaving – you do it every day or you wind
up looking like a bum.
    Jack Kemp, American football player and Republican
    congressman

We count on winning. And if we lose, don't beef. And the
best way to prevent beefing is – don't lose.
    Knute Rockne, football coach

If winning isn't everything, why do they keep score?
    Anon.

It matters not whether you win or lose; what matters is
whether *I* win or lose.
    Darrin Weinberg, wit

Show me a good sportsman and I'll show you a player I'm
looking to trade.
    Leo Durocher, Major League Baseball infielder and
    manager

I took my defeat like a man. I blamed it on my wife!
    Anon.

There's nothing to winning, really. That is, if you happen to
be blessed with a keen eye and agile mind and no scruples
whatsoever.
    Alfred Hitchcock, film maker

If you can play as if it means nothing when it means everything, then you are hard to beat.

Steve Davis, snooker player

Winning is overrated. The only time it is really important is in surgery and war.

Al McGuire, basketball coach

WINTER SPORTS

I think my favorite sport in the Olympics is the one in which you make your way through the snow, you stop, you shoot a gun, and then you continue on. In most of the world, it is known as the biathlon, except in New York City, where it is known as winter.

Michael Ventre, *LA Daily News*

The dullest Olympic sport is curling, whatever 'curling' means.

Andy Rooney, American commentator

Curling is the only sport where they have to speed up the action replays.

A. A. Gill, journalist

Curling was invented in the sixteenth century by bored Scottish farm labourers who passed the time by pushing a frozen cow pat up and down icy rivers.

Gillian Harris, journalist

Curling is not a sport. I called my grandmother and told her she could win a gold medal because they have dusting in the Olympics now.

Charles Barkley, American basketball player

Curling is half sport, half housework.
   Clive James, TV critic

That's what I call the ultimate laxative!
   Otto Jelinek, Canadian Minister of State for Fitness, after
   trying out the luge course at the Winter Olympics

!!!I Just HAD MY FIRST BOBSLED cRaSH!!!!! God is
real. I saw him today and he said come back later.
   Lolo Jones, American Olympic hurdler turned bobsledder,
   2012, tweet

Then there's the luge, for which I have only one question:
what drunken German gynaecologist invented that sport?
What guy said, 'You know what? I want to dress like a
sperm, shove an ice skate in my ass and go balls first down
an ice chute. Ja, that would be fun!'
   Robin Williams, actor and comic

Luge strategy? Lie flat and try not to die.
   Tim Steeves, stand-up

We have lots of Eddie Edwards in Norway, but we never let
them jump.
   Torbjorn Yggeseth, Norwegian ski jumper

It takes skill and courage to ski down a hill at 80mph
dressed in nothing but lycra.
   Ronald White

I was thrown out of the ice skating rink today. Apparently,
they don't allow ice fishing.
   Kevin Nealon

See also: FIGURE SKATING, SKIING

WOMEN

Women need a firm bra, not one of the flimsy all-elastic ones. That's especially true if you have large breasts. Otherwise they'll bounce and you'll always be waiting for them to come down before you take your next step.
Nina Kuscsik, American distance runner

Italian men and Russian women don't shave before a race.
Eddy Ottoz, Italian sprinter

Incompetence should not be confined to one sex.
Bill Russell, center for the Boston Celtics, on females officiating in the NBA

Women are more honest and fair than men and they know how to catch a man cheating.
Larry Foote, Pittsburgh Steelers linebacker, on Shannon Eastin, the first woman to officiate in an NFL regular-season game, 2012

How come women don't play ice hockey? Millions of girls played field hockey and, God knows, women can skate. Maybe it's the teeth. Women have this vain, silly thing about losing their front teeth.
Danny Liebert, stand-up

If someone says tennis is not feminine, I say screw it.
  Rosie Casals, American tennis player

A horse doesn't know whether the rider on his back wears a dress or pants away from the track.
  Diane Crump, pioneering woman jockey

She kept up with the lads for fourteen pints, but then they started talking about football.
  Martin Kemp, entertainer

When middle-class people and women started going to matches I thought it's a shame that hooliganism had stopped because that used to keep them out.
  Frank Skinner, comedian, on football crowds

The reason women don't play football is because eleven of them would never wear the same outfit in public.
  Phyllis Diller, comedienne

Since the age of fourteen, I have dearly wanted to be regarded as a sex object. I am absolutely sick of being loved for my cooking, accurate spin bowling, ability to solve anagrams and obtain credit from bookmakers and yet there are women who profess to be fearful of the alternative.
  Jeffrey Bernard, columnist

Women jockeys are a pain. Jumping's a man's game. They are not built like us. Most of them are as strong as half a Disprin.
  Steve Smith Eccles, jockey and tipster

Women don't gamble as much as men because their total instinct for gambling is satisfied by marriage.

Germaine Greer, author and feminist

I'd rather have an accident than fall in love – that's how much I love motor racing.

Lella Lombardi, Italian Formula 1 racing driver

The Stronger Women Get, The More Men Love Football

Mariah Burton Nelson, book title

Watching women playing cricket is a bit like watching men knitting.

Len Hutton, Yorkshire and England batsman

WRESTLING

Professional wrestling's most mysterious hold is on its audience.
Luke Neely, poker player, 1953

I believe that professional wrestling is clean and everything else in the world is fixed.
Frank Deford, sportswriter and novelist

Professional wrestling is just rehearsed acrobatics. It's not the sort of thing you would let your children go to see.
Georg Hackenschmidt, strongman and wrestler

I don't know what it is but I can't look at Hulk Hogan and believe that he's the end result of millions and millions of years of evolution.
Jim Murray, sportswriter

If professional wrestling did not exist, could you come up with this idea? Could you envision the popularity of huge men in tiny bathing suits pretending to fight?
Jerry Seinfeld, comedian

Just the way it is spelled.
Mirian Tsalkalamanidze, freestyle Soviet wrestler, on how to pronounce his name

See also: BOXING, MIXED MARTIAL ARTS

MISCELLANEOUS

Bullfights are hugely popular because you can sit comfortably with a hot dog and possibly watch a man die.
    Albert Brooks, actor and writer

The only polite thing to do when engaged in sky diving, hang gliding, ice climbing or any other dangerous sport is to die. That's what everyone is waiting around for.
    P. J. O'Rourke, libertarian humorist

We've just heard that Belgium's tug of war team have been disqualified for pushing.
    Stuart Hall, BBC Radio 5 Live, 2000

Gliding is a team sport, up to the point at which you become airborne.
    Bill Scull, British gliding coach

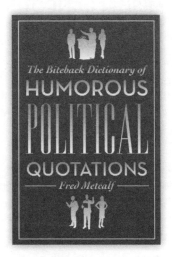